The Ele

GH00836321

INVENTORY BOOKS

www.inventorybooks.info

The Electric Information Age Book

MCLUHAN / AGEL / FIORE AND THE EXPERIMENTAL PAPERBACK

Jeffrey T. Schnapp
Adam Michaels

Princeton Architectural Press
New York

Foreword

Adam Michaels

Welcome to *The Electric Information Age Book*, the third volume of INVENTORY BOOKS, the paperback series that I initiated at Project Projects in 2009 and continue to edit and design. Seeking to advance the role of design as an integrated force in book editing and production, the series flouts perceived boundaries between form and content, using unconventional narrative modes, syntheses of texts and images, and context-specific typography—all as a means of revitalizing the space of the book to present critical content in an accessible, engaging format.

Despite this volume's tertiary position in the series, its subject matter represents an important origin point for INVENTORY BOOKS itself—indeed, the series title is derived from the subtitles of two books prominently featured here, both of which were produced by Jerome Agel, Quentin Fiore, and Marshall McLuhan.

The first of these books, *The Medium Is the Massage: An Inventory of Effects*, is one of very few objects that I've kept with me from childhood to the present day. Undoubtedly, this is due to Agel and Fiore's careful work producing an approachable, visually intensive translation of McLuhan's writing for a nonspecialist audience; the book's appeal to a range of ages must also be linked to its conceptual origin as a McLuhan book for children (see p. 49). Of equal importance, the book forged connections with a wide range of readers due to its creation for mass-market distribution, reaching diverse audiences well beyond its inception point in Midtown Manhattan—for example, arriving in the subculture-oriented paperback library gathered by my parents in 1960s–70s Chicago.

Accordingly, I had the opportunity to happen upon *The Medium Is the Massage* while foraging through my parents' bookshelves as a child. It was hidden in plain sight among the rows of well-read volumes of rock-and-roll criticism, science-fiction novels, and guides to various forms of Eastern spirituality, nearby stacks of yellowing issues of the *Whole Earth Catalog* and *Crawdaddy*. While I can't recall the precise moment of first grabbing *Massage* off the shelf, I certainly remember the book becoming an important part of my constellation of mind-expanding influences as a youth, as did the more overtly psychedelic *Rock and Other Four Letter Words* (see p. 201).

Under similar circumstances, *Massage* has endured its trip through the decades, maintaining a samizdat-like quality through the concealment of its conceptual innovations in an "ugly and ordinary" book format (in the positive sense formulated by Robert Venturi, Denise Scott Brown, and Steven Izenour in *Learning from Las Vegas*). Not only did this form provide the opportunity for the distribution of a best seller, it also created a strange kind of widespread archiving mechanism, in which one paperback might be maintained among many others, well after other artifacts of the '60s (mimeographed pamphlets, underground newspapers, brightly patterned clothing) would have either deteriorated or been disposed of.

Massage (and its successors, also explored in this volume) represents a powerful model for conveying complex content. Using simple, industry-standard means—offset printing in black ink; perfect binding in the mass-market paperback edition—Agel and Fiore produced a "non-book" (see pp. 85 and 107) for the masses, unlike anything ever seen outside of the rarefied milieus in which avant-garde typography has traditionally been produced and circulated.

If a *Massage*-like approach is technically possible for anyone endeavoring to write, design, typeset, print, and distribute a book, then one must wonder why the set of decades-old books shown here remains so exceptional amid the millions of books produced and distributed in the years since—especially given the advantages of today's readily accessible digital production tools. If not a question of technical means or exorbitant printing cost, the standardized form of most published material can reasonably be linked to the Fordist tendencies of the publishing industry's typical workflow. It's certainly more efficient to stick to standard operating procedure—writers write (often in isolation, with or without researchers), editors edit (quickly, under intensive time pressures), designers design (or, all too often, are barely able to, having received a limited commission at a late point in the book's process), printers print (quickly!), shippers ship (slowly, often across great distances), and eventually, booksellers sell (according to a set of circumscribed categories). Clearly, the operations of the publishing industry reflect a broader societal emphasis on specialization, spurred by the capitalist drive for profit—and thus publishing, one of the great engines of social communication, willingly sacrifices its capacity to produce exceptions for the sake of the ruthless efficiency of the norm.

One could further link the overriding sense of separation within publishing to pedagogical prejudices—specifically, the thorough division between an education in design and that in writing. Most educational superstructures ensure that the art student and the liberal arts student shall never meet. The alienation between text and image production is learned early on and reinforced by increased professionalization over the course of life.

However, venues do exist where this alienation is bridged. Within mainstream publishing, the children's book is perhaps the primary genre in which texts and images are allowed to fluidly intermingle. Ludic transgressions of formal boundaries are seemingly permissible for a young audience, whereas adults are expected to hunker down for the serious labor of textual reception (though they more frequently choose not to, already exhausted by the weightier matter of wage labor).

Outside of the publishing industry—far from anything like a strict workflow—an alternative tradition of subcultural publishing has thrived and continues to do so. From William Blake to William Morris, Kurt Schwitters to D. A. Levy, *The East Village Other* to *Touch & Go*, undercurrents of unconventional print communication methods have produced astounding objects and nurtured rich subcultures. However, these idealized forms of production tend to allow only for limited distribution—perhaps not a concern for the keepers of a self-contained avant-garde, but a source of frustration for anyone wishing to broadcast significant content to a diverse audience.

It's also worth noting that nearly every textual technique considered today to be a signifier of avant-garde book design (e.g., multiple narratives and annotation, marked by contrasting letterforms; complex columnar grids; usage of color for differentiation; integrated illustrations with text; unusual bindings; and so on) was already worked through centuries ago by scribes producing illuminated manuscripts—giving the lie to the contemporary importance of inward-looking experimentation.

I was reminded of the extraordinary qualities of illuminated manuscripts in February 2011, when attending the New York Public Library exhibition *Three Faiths*. Dozens of tantalizingly complex religious codices displayed an uncanny contemporaneity in their multivalent approaches to text. Midway through the exhibition, the Gutenberg Bible (1455) threw these books into sharp relief. Despite that book's intermittent ornamentation, one could readily observe the beginning of the brutal standardization brought about by the advent of movable type, implying something of a direct line toward today's warehouses stuffed with drab books consisting of seemingly identical gray page after gray page of uniform, justified text.

•　　　•　　　•

Amid heightened anxieties about the continued viability of the printed book, producers could do well to make use of the technology's latent potentials, embracing the book's intrinsic strengths as a site for synthesis and surprise, for materializing the dematerialized, and for distributing vital ideas beyond the bounds of the digital divide. Given contemporary tools, the methodical, hands-on, multimedia work of the scribe can be readily incorporated with the benefits of the age of technological reproducibility, namely the production and distribution of identical copies to a theoretically limitless audience.

To that end, the great lesson of *The Medium Is the Massage* and the other books featured here is that unconventional, intertwined content and form can be activated through widespread distribution as a means of creating profound connections with readers. I can certainly vouch for this, based upon my fortuitous childhood experiences stumbling upon some of these books. At best, these conditions provide a sense of new possibilities and alternative futures. For similar effect, one can look to mainstays such as Brecht in theater; Godard in film; the Minutemen in rock music; and, I hope, to the examples contained in this volume for book publishing.

Thus INVENTORY BOOKS takes inventory of the phenomena of our predecessors, both to report on what was possible in the Electric Information Age of the mid-1960s–mid-70s and to suggest some ways forward, toward a progressive approach to book production in our own time.

The
Cinematic
of
Paperback

Introduction

Steven Heller

Art

Books

Design inspiration comes when and where you least expect it. Mine was triggered by a slugfest with my co–art director at *ROCK*, a short-lived, late-'60s tabloid alternative-music magazine based in New York City. We were vehemently arguing about the efficacy of a certain anarchic layout technique he wanted to impose on my otherwise pristine modern design, when passions ran high and escalated to blows. Startled nonetheless by our atavistic behavior—we were peace-loving hippies, after all—and realizing the folly of our actions, we returned to our neutral corners and tried a more Woodstockian way to reconcile the disagreement. What happened next was the revelation that would in no small way alter my professional practice.

From under his desk my colleague pulled out two thin paperback books, which he believed would make his design argument less violent and more convincing. Handing them to me as though each were a pipe of peace, he proceeded to explain how their respective designs had deeply influenced him and were the inspiration for the magazine layouts over which our dispute had become ugly. The books were *War and Peace in the Global Village* by Marshall McLuhan and Quentin Fiore and *Do It!* by Jerry Rubin. Both volumes were designed by Fiore, whose name I had not heard before, yet whose work I would come to admire and respect.

As if touched by Tattypoo's wand (the Good Witch of the North in *The Wizard of Oz*), rather than creative adversaries, we became master and student. As the master slowly turned the pages, first of *War and Peace* then *Do It!,* he pointed out the various innovative elements of the design, including full-bleed high-contrast photographs; radical point shifts in text, headline, and pull-quote type; and visual elements laid out over contiguous spreads—taboo in traditional book composition. He especially pointed out in *Do It!,* Rubin's anti-establishment Yippie manifesto prior to his becoming an early investor in Apple Computers, the various silhouetted photographs that were repeated and cropped and mortised into the text, to give the illusion of flying or running from page to page. He noted the technique was rooted in cinematography. He also underscored the fact that these books were visual texts; in fact, it was possible, if not advisable, to engage with them by bifurcating the reading experience into visual and verbal. And as the reader became used to the format, the two components would become a single totality.

My former adversary's apparent reverence for these books—and palpable joy when explaining Fiore's talents—lulled him into a state of nirvana. Me? I was just happy not to be exchanging knuckle punches. Yet, as noted above, this was a real eye-opener.

"These books are like magazines," I said.

"Yes. But they are more," he insisted. "They are films between covers. Not just storyboards, but kinetically composed pacing that forces the eye and mind to follow text and picture in ways that are unique for books." His ethereal musings on the anatomy of Fiore's designs stuck with me because I was fascinated by the idea that flat design on paper could appear to move. And Fiore managed to expertly achieve that in a small-format paperback book. Had I been introduced to the Messiah?

I immediately went out and bought *War and Peace* and *Do It!* (dog-eared copies of which I still have in my library), but also found Fiore's better-known opus, the paperback edition of McLuhan's *The Medium Is the Massage* (years later I acquired the hardcover edition). "Produced" by Jerome Agel, a freelance book packager who had a yen for experimentation and producing books-as-performance, *Massage* was a veritable bible for the electric-information-media-age generation. Subtitled *An Inventory of Effects*, it was a prescient approach to book content in an era when television was stealing popular attention away from magazines and books. Between the graphic effects, McLuhan, the shaman of alternative-media culture, sprinkled his philosophical aphorisms and prognostications—many of which underpin today's new media experiences.

Massage was a graphic Pandora's box. But instead of releasing evils into the world when opened, it provided countless ways to compose, arrange, and make content. It was no accident that Fiore's name appeared under McLuhan's as coauthor. His visual language was an equal, if not dominant, contribution to the book. Without Fiore's input, there would be no book.

Yet as I delved deeper into the myth of *Massage* and other McLuhan tomes, I found that not everyone accepted his pronouncements as THE WORD. The *New York Times* book critic Eliot Fremont-Smith refused to give an iota of credence to McLuhan and, by extension, Fiore: "As everybody knows, Herbert Marshall McLuhan came to Earth in a flying saucer around 1965, lugging with him the Tablets of the new Electric Age. 'Get thee behind me, typographical man,' they were inscribed; 'Thou shalt not be linear in thought, word or deed for the medium is the message and the world is a global village to be apprehended through electric circuitry which is an extension of the central nervous system.'"Calling McLuhan's work "hokus pokus," he dismissed it as repetitive, crankish, and disjointed, "and, perhaps to cover borrowings of familiar findings in other fields (e.g., psychoanalysis), frenzied.... He seems increasingly busy, not in extending his original insights about the metaphorical nature of our perception and communication of reality and the way new technologies have altered the metaphors but in transposing his insights into static epigrams." Wherein, he sent a grenade into Fiore's foxhole.

"*War and Peace in the Global Village* is a collection of these," rails Fremont-Smith, "plus lots of pictures (hockey players, Napoleon returning from Russia, Einstein sticking his tongue out) and lots of quotes (from all over, but mostly from *Finnegans Wake*) both in the text proper and in the margins. In 'mosaic' layout, production and authorship, it is a companion to last year's *The Medium Is the Massage: An Inventory of Effects*. The new book, described as 'an inventory of some of the current spastic situations that could be eliminated by more feedforward,' revolves around the central idea that war is a result of the anxiety aroused when changing metaphors of perception fail to yield up familiar self-images."[1]

Fremont-Smith was not the lone skeptic; there were many others in the literary and media worlds who couldn't see McLuhan's future. However, negative reviews by the keepers of establishment standards (although Fremont-Smith later moved on from the *Times* to the more radical *Village Voice*) simply added more credibility to McLuhan's ideas and Fiore's graphic translations of them. In fact, there were possibly just as many fans who saw greater prescience than faddish philosophizing in these books.

An unsigned précis to one of Fiore's visual essays titled "The Future of the Book,"[2] which has a decidedly close relationship to such book art as Tom Phillips's *A Humument*, offered this description: "[His] elliptical and cryptic style…stimulates all the perceptual senses in a new way. The changing style of life in the age of computer technology is forcing people to alter their perceptual styles to even the most commonplace things of their environment." The writer goes on to say, as if he or she were writing in today's media environment: "Such a world alters the most commonplace things, like the publishing of books. Publishing companies are now being acquired by the major electronic giants such as Xerox and RCA. Publishing houses who once published books are now going to publish information, but it will be instantaneous information. Here mass media and TV becomes central."[3]

In an interview I conducted with Fiore in the mid-1980s, he admitted that he was actually most proud of his "classical" book design using traditional hot metal type. Nonetheless, he strongly believed in experimentation and was not just attempting to navigate through McLuhan's disjointed prognostications, sarcastically mocked by Fremont-Smith: he was actually attempting to construct what eventually evolved into a primitive iteration of the "information super highway," using the paperback book as its bedrock or foundation. In my interview he explained, "I was always interested in simple technologies, hand technologies." The reason for his experiments was to have "a dialogue between the computer and the book." Fiore had made some educational films for Bell Laboratories, which certainly factored into his desire to stretch the page and the book in a more kinetic fashion. "I began to think in terms of forms other than the accepted form. Playing around with visual axes and sequential presentations." Referring to *Massage* as a prime example of his approach, he noted, "It reduces very, very complicated, complex ideas into simple signs, glyphs, patches of text, and so on, and this is what I intended it to be." And why, aside from the formal reasons and technological mandates, was he doing this? "There was the Vietnam war. There were new forms of expression. There was the Free Speech Movement. You name it and this was the world," he said.

•　　•　　•

I wanted to be Fiore. Or rather I wanted to find ways to design books and magazines where the visual language was as important to the content as the text. Before Fiore, my inspiration was *Eros* and *Avant Garde* magazine designer Herb Lubalin's expressive and illustrative typography. After Fiore, typo-pictorial narratives were the answer to the question "what's next?" As it happened, in my case, it was harder to make a book into a magazine (especially a tabloid one) than a magazine into a book— although I tried.

At nineteen years old, much to my surprise, I was hired as art director of *Evergreen Review*, which only a few years earlier was a highly innovative, left-wing magazine of art, culture, and politics. By the time I was brought on, the magazine and the Grove Press empire had fallen on hard times. In fact, the large, full-color newsstand version of *Evergreen*, known for its taboo-busting visual and textual content, had folded, and a year or so later was revived as a paperback book. I was to design the paperback. What serendipity! The recent awakening to the wonder of paperback publishing was fresh in my mind. So when asked to take the art directorial helm, I was already inspired by Fiore-isms and raring to put them in motion.

My own attempt, however, was nothing like his; rather it was a pitiful attempt at mimicry. Mastering the mass-market paperback size was not as easy as it looked. So I turned to another model that was more in keeping with my own aesthetics: *US: A Paperback Magazine*, edited for three issues between 1969 and 1970 by the former *Village Voice* rock critic Richard Goldstein. *US* was a bona fide book-a-zine; a radical size-shift from the tabloid-scale underground newspapers, which it was more or less emulating yet also distancing itself from. My entire career up until that time was with underground "tabs."

The first three issues of *US* sought to condense underground, alternative culture concerns into a mass-market product that would be sold on racks in an attempt to attract a larger, more national youth audience. It failed to attract a sizable enough following, but it was a valiant attempt and a standard of design and visual content I also hoped to emulate, which I did with enthusiasm, although, again, not with great success.

My two issues as art director/designer of the *Evergreen Review* may not have been innovative or inspirational like Fiore's books or *US*, but they perpetuated the idea that paperbacks could be more than just tightly packed wide columns of text. They could have typographic variety and visual buoyancy. They could be as wonderful to read as to hold. My *Evergreen*s were okay, but my second opportunity to be the next Fiore was on the horizon.

Grove Press's Publisher and Editor in Chief Barney Rosset, who was the first to import and be arrested for such contraband erotic films as *I Am Curious (Yellow)*, decided to publish a book and tabloid newsprint magazine of essays on Bernardo Bertolucci's *Last Tango in Paris*, starring Marlon Brando as a middle-aged hotel owner who, mourning the death of his wife, gets involved in a steamy relationship with a younger woman. The film's raw portrayal of sexual violence led to international censorship. Rosset secured the screenplay and actual excerpts from the film. I was given a pile of 35 mm filmstrips to convert into stills for black-and-white reproduction in the book. The kinetic opportunities were awesome—although simply running contiguous strips does not a cinematic book make. Again, I realized what Fiore accomplished with his radical scale changes, conversion of halftone to high-contrast photos, and typographic pyrotechnics, which were all essential to making the small-paperback format perceptively larger. Transforming the paperback into a veritable mammoth screen was the trick—the magic was massaging the medium into the message.

The *Tango* book was an opportunity to play with as many of Fiore's effects as I had the capacity to produce. And one boon was a new graphic arts machine called the Stat King, a combination Photostat camera and printer (about the size of one of today's Smart cars). It was so easy to use—and to make all kinds of stats and screen prints and veloxes—that even a technodope like me could produce quirky effects. I was fortunate enough to have constant access to the Stat King, and made high-contrast and continuous line-screen art to my heart's content.

Having the means of preproduction in the designer's hands was a kind of emancipation that prefigured the greater license triggered by desktop publishing. Being able to instantly play with special and routine effects increased the design options tenfold. Little did we know in the early '70s that the personal computer would make it one hundredfold. Another plus was being able to actually photostat (on glossy or matte paper) the pages as actual size. Making a "dummy" enabled the designer to modulate the pacing of the pages efficiently and alter the component parts effectively. In retrospect, these were primitive techniques and technologies. But design—as prefigured in Fiore's paperbacks—was just waiting for the next big technology to enable the next big thing(s).

The *Tango* paperback was destined for the shredder. Grove Press was already in trouble, sinking steadily into a financial abyss. Rosset released the book to little fanfare. He also used the same content for a simultaneous tabloid newsprint version of the book—for what reason I don't know. During a trip to a bookseller's convention in California, the original mechanicals for the book were thrown out by accident, and all of the text had to be re-created through photostats, which I fortuitously had made as a record. This mishap marked the last time I worked on a paperback of this kind.

Throughout the late '60s and early '70s the concept of what a book is was morphing to conform to many stimuli. Paperbacks, once a second or third bastard cousin to the hardcover, were now accepted as a legitimate venue for serious literature and scholarship. It was also an economical way to produce books. That it became an art/design venue for a brief time opened up the publishing world to many more possibilities.

Oh, by the way, the McLuhan/Fiore books are still around, and David Carson redesigned some of the recent edition covers. That's right, the same Carson whose "end of print" prognostication was met with a certain sarcasm in the 1990s but is now talked about quite seriously, even among longtime publishers.

An Inven of Inven

tory

tories

Greetings!

Come on in.

...an inventory?

Yes, this book is an inventory.
(But of a distinctive kind.)

It provides an itemization, history, and detailed account of a set of cultural objects produced between the mid-1960s and the mid-1970s, during the heyday of what was then referred to as the television, or the electric information, age. The objects in question are heterogeneous. Only occasionally have they been seen as forming a cohesive set. Yet they possess a core of shared traits.

The purpose of this inventory is to draw a circle around a body of objects; to take stock of their common properties; and to tell a story about where they came from, what they were, and where they led. Their variety is such as to sustain a multiplicity of narrative threads: about the rise of a new photo-driven graphic vernacular; about the triumph of a certain cognitive/cultural style; about criss-crossings between high and low, the erudite and the mass cultural; about the shifting boundaries between books, magazines, music, television, and film.

So what you will encounter here is less THE story than ONE story of a rearrangement of the field of mass communications whose impact can still be felt in the present.

...of inventories?

Affirmative, again.

The word *inventory* points toward two subtitles that launched the genre of print artifacts being accounted for here: *An Inventory of Effects* and *An inventory of some of the current spastic situations that could be eliminated by more feedforward*. Both were attached to mass-market paperbacks signed "Marshall McLuhan, Quentin Fiore" and "co-ordinated by Jerome Agel." Both works surveyed technology's impact on the contemporary psyche and society. In neither does the word *inventory* occur internally. The term is restricted to the title page in order to proclaim and frame the birth of a new publishing genre: the electric information age book. For purposes of concision, I refer to such books as "INVENTORY BOOKS."

INVENTORY BOOKS put themselves forward as alternatives to traditional books, faulted by their detractors for approaching today's tasks with yesterday's concepts and tools. Fast-paced verbal-visual collages, intermedia hybrids, nonlinear **"COLLIDE-O-SCOPIC"** look-arounds aimed squarely at the contemporary scene and at younger readers, INVENTORY BOOKS made the rhythmic sequencing, layering, and interleaving of photographic-textual combinations their stock and trade.

INVENTORY BOOKS share a loose parentage with various avant-garde predecessors and peers, from futurism to Fluxus; a parentage sometimes acknowledged on their pages. But their vocation was, from the outset, mainstream and down-market. They assumed the form of inexpensive, swiftly produced paperback originals animated by the chatter of the marketplace and the street, and always rough around the (graphic) edges.

INVENTORY BOOKS belong to a large publishing family that includes press books for promoting movies, instant and current event books, news and fashion magazines, television series books, and counterculture rags. During the 1960s and 1970s they circulated under many labels: documentaries, paperback magazines, talk-rock albums, synergistic collages, photo-essays, and collections. Some were crafted to make demanding content intelligible and attractive to a mass readership; others sought to promote political causes or to support a given media or music subculture.

...but why?

If this book inventories a corpus of *historical* materials, the ultimate horizon toward which it looks is the media landscape of the present. Just as its design dialogues with the objects inventoried, its narrative toggles between the (digital) present and the (televisual) past. The tale that it tells—sometimes explicitly, more often implicitly—is of genealogical continuities.

...how so?

The core of "An Inventory of Inventories" consists in reconstructing eight books developed by Agel, initially in collaboration with the graphic designer Fiore. Most are **"COMPREHENSIVE CONTRACTIONS"**—the phrase is Agel's—of the writings of contemporary thinkers such as Marshall McLuhan, R. Buckminster Fuller, Herman Kahn, and Carl Sagan. Agel also described them as books "designed to put into popular form, or into more understandable form, some of the great ideas of our time."[1] Others described them as **"A SMALL SHELF OF VOLUMES DESIGNED TO TURN IMPORTANT BUT NOT-SO-EASY-TO-UNDERSTAND IDEAS INTO READING THE AVERAGE MAN WILL ENJOY."**[2]

The series debuts in 1967 with the publication of *The Medium Is the Massage*, which serves as the centerpiece of the present account. It concludes in 1975 with Agel's collaboration with Alan Lakein, *It's About Time & It's About Time*. In reconstructing the genesis and development of the sequence, the present essay combines attention to the books' context with analysis of their content.

Five smaller circles have been drawn around clusters of works from the same period that hover along the edges of the central narrative. These overlap to varying degrees with the larger circle drawn in "An Inventory of Inventories." The first, labeled **photo•essayism**, examines John Berger's amalgamations of the verbal and photographic essay. The second, **album•art**, surveys books that seek to mime films or records. The third, entitled **magazine•book**, tracks experiments with periodicals in the form of paperbacks. Entitled **agit•pop**, the fourth looks at iterations of the book qua militant pamphlet or manifesto. The fifth, **shelf•help**, concerns electric information age books of the self. As the section titles hint, each cluster stands for a distinctive publishing typology.

```
Dear Mr. Agel: I am three and
one-half years old. You're right.

[name withheld at the parents'
request]
Champlain, New York
```

**the typophoto governs the tempo of
the new visual literature...**

The twentieth century was launched under the aegis of two total concepts of the book.

The first is distant from the noisy, news-edged world of INVENTORY BOOKS. It was articulated by the symbolist poet Stéphane Mallarmé in his essay "The Book, A Spiritual Instrument." It dreamed of the entire universe flowing into **a single total book**: a book, both material and metaphysical, in time and outside time, that would fulfill and transcend the revolution inaugurated by Johannes Gutenberg.

The second brings us closer to the world of electric information age books. It was embraced by early avant-gardes such as futurism and dreamed of an exploded, porous book whose every page could become an all-comprehending theater of the present and a staging ground for ever-surprising futures. László Moholy-Nagy is but one early theorist of this **Book of the Now**:

> Until recently typeface and typesetting rigidly preserved a technique which, admittedly, guaranteed the purity of the linear effect, but ignored the new dimensions of life. Only quite recently has there been typographic work which uses the contrasts of typographic material ... in an attempt to establish a correspondence with modern life. These efforts have, however, done little to relax the inflexibility that has hitherto existed in typographic practice. An effective loosening-up

can be achieved only by the most sweeping and all-embracing use of the techniques of photography, zincography, the electrotype, etc. The flexibility and elasticity of these techniques bring with them a new reciprocity between economy and beauty. With the development of photo-telegraphy, which enables reproductions and accurate illustrations to be made instantaneously, **even philosophical works will presumably use the same means**, though on a higher plane, as the present day American magazines. The form of these new typographic works will, of course, be quite different typographically, optically, and synoptically from the linear typography of today.[3]

The passage is from Moholy-Nagy's earliest Bauhaus treatise, *Painting Photography Film*, published in 1925. However visionary, the loosening up that it promotes became the shared undertaking of multiple generations and categories of practitioners. The spectrum was wide: some were professional designers and artists, others journeymen; some worked for illustrated newspapers, publishers, or commercial printing shops, others labored in the laboratories of the avant-garde. There was little agreement on terminology. **TYPOPHOTOGRAPHY** was the neologism Moholy-Nagy coined to denote **the flexible, elastic, photo-driven medium of the future**. Jan Tschichold opted for the umbrella phrase **THE NEW TYPOGRAPHY** (with the understanding that  we "see in photography exactly the factor that distinguishes our typography from everything that went before").[4] Commercially minded peers would instead have identified the venture with *a* **new age of advertising**, with the making of **the modern magazine**, or with emerging genres of reportage like the **photo chronicle**.

Various labels and genre designations came and went over the century. But not a core conviction: that offset lithography, photography, telegraphy, telephony, radio, moving pictures (and, later, video, television, and electronic data networks), shaped by and shaping, in turn, new social needs and expectations, had disrupted the galaxy of the Gutenbergian book and created the preconditions for a communications revolution. A gulf had opened up between the printed page—with its well-oiled typographic geometries, its subordination of image to text, and a cognitive linearity that it both produced and enforced—and contemporary life, with its simultaneity, accelerated cadences, and overloaded sensorium. The solution was to reestablish what Moholy-Nagy calls "a correspondence": to bridge the gulf through a faster, freer, more compact, and attention-grabbing mode of communication, a mode better suited to the requirements of an era in which the multitudes were history's (distracted) masters. In short, **to forge a new verbal-visual vernacular**.

The photograph quickly establishes itself as the normative semiotic unit and the filmstrip as the standard narrative frame within the new vernacular. Text is recast in a multiplicity of leading and supporting roles (logos, headlines, captions), configured as one visual element among others within an overall geometric mesh. The labyrinthine logic of syntax yields to **a simplified universal grammar of cuts and pastes**. The printed page, once detached from the present, now edges closer, thanks to the near instantaneity with which its contents can be transmitted, not to mention composed and disseminated. If the total Book of the Now still lies somewhere over the horizon, its imminent advent is confirmed by the periodical press: "present day American magazines," writes Moholy-Nagy, "are already putting into practice new typophotographical forms. Someday, these will encompass works of science and substance, making them accessible to mass audiences: *even philosophical works will presumably use the same means.*"

PRESUMABLY SO.

But for the next few decades, the periodical press would soldier on as the chief agent of graphic innovation, whether within the orbit of limited-distribution architecture, graphics, art, and design reviews; mainstream political periodicals like *USSR in Construction* and *La rivista illustrata del Popolo d'Italia*; or mass-market magazines such as America's *Life* or imitators like *Tempo* in Italy. Books, not to mention "philosophical works," remained tethered to tradition.

an implacable book

There are exceptions, of course. Few were more influential than Charles Édouard Jeanneret's reworking of a series of prior writings from *L'esprit nouveau* into the 1923 book-manifesto *Vers une architecture*, a collaboration with the Purist painter Amédée Ozenfant that marks the former's debut under the name Le Corbusier.

Prophetic and aphoristic in tone, incantatory in its repetitions, peppered with paradoxes, provocations, and injunctions, *Vers une architecture* drives a wedge into the foundations of the architectural establishment. In so doing, it casts a sidelong eye toward broader audiences. The accompanying marketing pamphlet declared that it was "**not intended only for professionals…but made instead for the general public.**" "Just out," read the banner headline on its lead page, with the inscription below: **THIS BOOK IS IMPLACABLE, IT IS UNLIKE ANY OTHER**.[5] To a degree, it was.

The promised nonresemblance of *Vers une architecture* to conventional books refers to the verbal-visual strategies that animate the book. These begin with its cover: a flat, simplified geometric design composed of capitalized sans serif titles of variable size and density printed against a pale blue backdrop within an outer and inner white frame. The outer frame mirrors the book's edge; the inner frame contains a black-and-white photograph: a cen-tered, deeply receding view of the lateral corridor of the steamship Empress of Asia, the first ocean liner to feature movies as a form of passenger entertainment.[6]

The gesture is self-reflexive. It identifies *Vers une architecture* with passage on a work of naval architecture. It equates the act of reading with that of walking down a gallery that invites linear motion (reading) but also looking to the left and to the right at framed openings onto a seascape and into the ship's interiors (viewing picture sequences). Last but not least, it associates the title's promise of movement *toward* an architecture—an architecture soon to be revealed as an architecture of movement inspired by automobiles, aircraft, and steamships—with a floating city, some of whose interior walls have been converted into supports for projecting motion pictures.

Though not yet integrally typophotographic, *Vers une architecture* relies on the playful interlacing of arguments made typographically in the text's main narrative with arguments developed through image-caption sequences. The former work with alternating wide and narrow headlines, boldfacing and italics, and the spatial isolation of recurring slogans and chapter syntheses; the latter, as confirmed by Le Corbusier's meticulous preparatory sketches, establish tightly choreographed rhythmic and formal patterns, reinforced through the cropping and altering of photographs. Shifts in scale and orientation prevail on both fronts, conferring on the book a double identity, half filmstrip, half Mallarméian roll of the dice, placed in the service of a single hortatory purpose: the dramatic

staging of a dilemma ("architecture or revolution") and its resolution ("revolution can be avoided").

~~illustration~~ (*nein danke*)

Other photo-driven books issued calls to action in the wake of Le Corbusier's. In late Weimar Germany, they surfaced in the form of book-length "essays" in which an argument is made by photographic means alone, as in Franz Roh and Jan Tschichold's *Foto-Auge* (*Photo-Eye*) and August Sander's *Antlitz der Zeit* (*Face of Our Time*), both published in 1929. (Tschichold's early 1930s designs of socially engaged books for the working masses represent a complementary endeavor.)

The chronology is slightly later in the United States, where most such experiments were cast in a documentarist mold whose success during the 1930s was cemented by newsreels and consolidated by photo magazines like

Life. These so-called **documentary books** have roots that extend back to pioneering experiments in political photojournalism like Jacob Riis's *How the Other Half Lives: Studies among the Tenements of New York* (1890). They come into their own as a distinctive genre after the Great Depression with the publication of Erskine Caldwell and Margaret Bourke-White's *You Have Seen Their Faces* (1937), Dorothea Lange and Paul Taylor's *An American Exodus: A Record of Human Erosion* (1939), James Agee and Walker Evans's *Let Us Now Praise Famous Men* (1941), and Richard Wright, Dorothea Lange, Walker Evans, and Arthur Rothstein's *12 Million Black Voices: A Folk History of the Negro in the United States* (1941). All are works that, rather than fuse the photographic and the textual/typographical, treat them as separate realms, each with its distinctive dignity. "**The photographs are not illustrative,**" writes Evans. "**They, and the text, are coequal, mutually independent, and fully collaborative.**"[7]

Coequality means that the photographs in documentary books are typically gathered into freestanding signatures that sit at the edge of a conventionally typeset narrative that rarely if ever directly refers to them. To mark their autonomy, they often precede the title page and text. Sometimes they are paired with nonillustrative captions, as in *You Have Seen Their Faces*, where fictionalized but plausible place names and utterances appear unaccompanied by proper names: "No person, place, or episode in this book is fictitious, but names and places have been changed so as to avoid unnecessary individualization."[8] The final phrase is telling, for the documentary book is, at once, hyperfactual and above fact, radically individualizing and deindividualizing. It plumbs the depths of visual and verbal particularity, caressing every craggy cranny of a weathered landscape, object, utterance, or face. But its aim is always **to transfigure a mass of particulars into a mass epic and mosaic composed of the everyday** sacrifices and struggles of ordinary citizens.

Affirming the value of photography and narrative as art rather than as news or fungible raw material, documentary books flow into the photo-essayist and the agitpop streams of 1960s publishing. They diverge from the scrappy, synthetic pop style of INVENTORY BOOKS, whose origins lie less in fine art than in the art of advertising.

the producer

The inventor of INVENTORY BOOKS, Jerome Agel (1930–2007), had a keen appreciation for photography and narrative as fine arts. But he was, first and foremost, a journalist equipped with a mile-a-minute, omnivorous mind and a genius for public relations. A native of Burlington, Vermont, and graduate of the University of Vermont and the Columbia School of Journalism, Agel had been a sportswriter during his precollegiate years. His post-Columbia career began with a stint at the *New York Construction News*, followed by work in the public relations department at Merritt-Chapman & Scott and then by an extended tenure at Batten, Barton, Durstine & Osborn, the New York advertising agency, where his most significant assignment was a project that prefigures certain features of INVENTORY BOOKS: the organization of an outreach event known as Chicago Dynamic Week. Sponsored by U.S. Steel and held October 27–November 2, 1957, with the aim of dramatizing the city's architectural and building heritage (and burying the memory of the recent Calumet Park race riots), Chicago Dynamic sought to place architecture at the center of the public conversation through a multimedia blitz combining tours, workshops, television and radio broadcasts, vocational sessions for high school students, and official dinners that involved both local dig-

nitaries and guests of honor like Frank Lloyd Wright. Alistair Cooke, the host of CBS's *Omnibus*, the first network television series dedicated to the arts, was invited to host one of the evenings. Carl Sandburg, already the author of several poems on the Windy City, was commissioned to compose a new work to mark the occasion.[9] The event was put together not thanks to social connections but to Agel's agile use of what would remain his preferred networking tool: the telephone. (As fate would have it, his future collaborator Fiore designed the numbers on the dial of the standard Bell telephone.)

Agel never made his peace with the staid culture of the publishing industry and, by the late 1950s, had founded a public relations partnership. In the early 1960s he ran his own independent office, counting among his clients the cosmetics firm Fabergé. The Agel Publishing Company was incorporated in January 1964. As a publisher, Agel belonged to a new tribe of entrepreneurs who first began to have a decisive impact on the publishing scene during the 1950s. Known as "packagers," "copublishers," and "producers," these new figures set about conceiving and putting together books on a contract basis with existing publishing houses, rather than operating from within. Though their products ran the gamut from up-market to down-market, they were often edgy or unconventional books with print runs of over one hundred thousand. The novelist Eileen Lottman profiles them as follows in the *Village Voice*:

> What's a book producer? According to Jerome Agel, who seems to be the only one around with that title, he writes, edits, designs, lays out, makes up the mechanicals to deliver to the various publishers he contracts with (makes up his own contracts, too), and gets a byline as producer along with collaborators who do the heavy lifting about the subject matter, like Marshall McLuhan, Buckminster Fuller, and Herman Kahn. The books are published as paperback originals, get the full mass-market treatment, and the "producer" pitches in with the ads and promotion, too. It's a kind of old-world craftsmanship in conglomerationland.[10]

Agel did devise his own distinctive model of book production. But he was not alone. His peers were a small but heterogeneous group. They included men like Lawrence Lamm in the domain of practical manuals and

George Rainbird in the art book sector. Working with the typographer Ruari McLean between 1951 and 1958, Rainbird designed and produced accessible illustrated books that set new quality standards for integrating image and text. The other end of the spectrum included the likes of Lyle Kenyon Engel, founder of the "novel factory" **BOOK CREATION, INC.**, which churned out hundreds of books a year in the form of pseudonymously authored series such as *The Kent Family Chronicles*, *The Bastard*, *Australians*, *White Indian Series*, *Wagons West*, and *Stagecoach*. And they included Bernard Geis, the founder of Bernard Geis Associates, who perfected the art of the celebrity book, best remembered for sexed-up best sellers like Helen Gurley Brown's *Sex and the Single Girl*, Jacqueline Susann's *Valley of the Dolls*, and the advice books of the "happy hooker" Xaviera Hollander.

Advertising was generally viewed as an afterthought in the button-down, gentlemen's profession of publishing. Books were imagined as self-sufficient artifacts, able to find their readership through press reviews and word of mouth. In a polemic with Roger Straus (of Farrar Straus), Agel dubbed book advertising "consistently dull and lackluster. Only in the rarest instance do book ads convey the enthusiasm and dedication of the writer, publisher or editor."[11] The packagers/producers developed an alternative vision. For them **a book was a media event, to be promoted before, during, and after the moment of publication**. And a book was *business*. Geis routinely assigned $100,000 publicity budgets to each of his books (a considerable sum in the 1960s) and devised custom-tailored campaigns. In the case of Henry Sutton's novel *The Voyeur*, for example, Geis had peep show displays installed in Grand Central and Penn Station. A risqué billboard appeared in Times Square where, on February 6, 1969, the star of all these initiatives, Sarah

Smithers, featured on the book's cover (not to mention the covers of numerous nudie magazines), performed an impromptu striptease. The twenty-three-year-old daughter of the former British secretary of foreign affairs—a "socialite turned sexpot," according to Geis's ad campaign—was arrested and then released by the police; Geis was indicted for blocking traffic and "conducting a street fair without a permit."[12] But the exploit landed *The Voyeur* on the pages of the *New York Times*.

These sorts of stunts built on a revolution that had already begun transforming publishing into a modern industry during the 1930s. The pioneers were firms like Doubleday and Pocket Books. The first moved its operations from Manhattan to Long Island to reduce costs, embarked on a campaign of takeovers to expand its stable of authors and backlists, developed subscription readerships through the Literary Guild and the Dollar Book Club (both Doubleday properties), promoted mail-order sales, and built up the world's first chain of publisher-owned bookstores. The second invented the twenty-five-cent paperback and **the instant book**: Pearl Buck's novel *The Good Earth* (1939) inaugurated the enormously successful former series; Donald Porter Geddes's album *Franklin Delano Roosevelt: A Memorial* (1945) launched the latter (the book was out less than a week after FDR's death). Pocket Books were distributed via magazine wholesalers, which meant a distribution chain that included newsstands, variety stores, drugstores, and even bus and train stations.[13] Among the first to understand the significance of the change was McLuhan, who as early as *Explorations 2* observed that "the pocket book takes the hex out of culture. In our particular milieu, it is a new *form* of communication."[14] He completed the thought a decade later in *Understanding Media*, calling "the phenomenon of the paperback, the book in

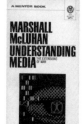

'cool' version" the mark of television's "transformation of book culture into something else.... **The paperback itself has become a vast mosaic world in depth**, expressive of the changed sense-life of Americans, for whom depth experience in words, as in physics, has become entirely acceptable, and even sought after."[15]

what's *really* happening...

The paperback revolution narrowed the gulf between publishing and contemporary media culture. But *Publishers Weekly*, the industry's main organ, remained in the hands of the old guard, and venues such as *Book World* and the *New York Times Book Review* were limited to reviewing new books. "What about the social scene, the backstage, the emerging trend lines, the rumors, the buzz of ideas?" wondered Agel one morning, razor in hand: "**Books are really part of show business**." Soon thereafter, in early 1964, he set about the task of launching his own tabloid-sized monthly titled *Books,* with himself as editor, publisher, and promoter.[16] The review's subtitles bespeak its iconoclastic, playful spirit: *The Monthly Misnomer, The Lively One,* and *the newspaper for people who read books*. All are indicative of Agel's goal of transforming the book world's cocktail parties, contracts, politics, glam, and gossip into a spirited public conversation.

Agel ran small eye-catching ads for *Books* in the *New York Times*, scrawled as if a napkin sketch animated by doodles. Most contained subscription coupons that were deliberately flipped and handwritten notes written upside down. They read "BOO AGEL!" (as if denunciatory rather than promotional), with the missing *KS* downsized to reinforce a concluding play on words: "Send us the coupon today. It's the kindest cut of all." Flirting with scandal, the ads dubbed *Books* "our advertising agency"—at a time when Agel was known mostly in advertising circles—and promised an irreverent mix.[17]

Our Advertising Agency

By JEROME AGEL, Editor of a Monthly Misnomer

Every month we put out a lively newspaper for the literate reader with a sense of humor. In spite of our agency, we're a roaring success.

We cover What's Happening. Who's Happening. Underground. Overground. Long before anyone else, usually.

We call ourselves "BOOKS." Our readers call us other things. Like, "BOOKS the damn thing I can't put down until I have read everything in it—twice." "BOOKS my sophisticated LSD cube." "BOOKS the funniest, hippest thing I've ever read." "BOOKS my monthly brunch coat."

While reviewers are praising for the umpteenth time the diary of a Swiss private and the history of glass design, we're reporting what's happening, what's *really* happening, baby. Our theory is that books, authors, films, viable ideas—people—aren't as dull as others make them out to be.

Highlights from our monthly psychodrama:

—Idaho's homosexual scandals, "The Boys of Boise."

—The real message of Barbara Garson's "MacBird": "Don't jump on the RFK bandwagon."

—Marshall McLuhan: "Art is anything you can get away with."

—Tom Wolfe, why *do* you dress that way? Tom Wolfe, why do you *dress* that way?

—For Hotch the Belle Tolls.

—"Best Minds in Medicine Are Taking Care of Rabbits."

—Jeane Dixon, the seer: "Governor Wallace would make a good President."

—The new journalist is replacing the old novelist.

—One of Truman Capote's "In Cold Blood" killers, Perry Smith, sounds likewell, like Holden Caulfield: "She was trying hard to act casual and friendly. I really liked her. She was really nice." And. "Now, that's something I despise. Anybody that can't control themselves sexually. Christ, I hate that kind of stuff." On the piano rack in the Clutter farmhouse that night was the music for "Coming Thru the Rye."

Every issue is an unpredictable experience. News, seminal ideas, layouts available nowhere else. Plus plus plus. Scoop scoop scoop. Up to 75 per cent of our readers have re-subscribed—unprecedented interest! *Trendmaker, trendmaker, make me a trend.*

Another important and original service: Summaries of hundreds of hardcover and paperback books in the month they are published, by category.

Write the beautiful people: "Terrific, lively writing, sensational illustrations. Reading BOOKS is like living with someone you love." "Like a great night at the movies or theatre." "Loved your topless issue." "Fantastically imaginative, entertaining, insightful. Scholarly books never had it so good. Put me down for two more gift subscriptions." Writes Newsweek in a two-thirds of a page rave: "BOOKS has a talent for first-rate scoops." Writes James Purdy: "How can you last? Isn't America beautiful enough without you?"

BOOKS is available *only* by subscription. Not on newsstands. If you want to be included, send us the coupon today. It's the kindest cut of all.

BOOKS/Agel Publishing Co.
598 Madison Ave., NYC 10022

One year: $2.92 ($2.92?)
Two years: $5.50.

Books combined the characteristics of an industry insider report with humor, opinion pieces, reporting on contemporary pop culture, and commentary on current events with an emphasis on sexuality, social justice, women's rights, and contemporary media. But at its core it was a high-level literary review, whose mix of authors included Tom Wolfe, Saul Bellow, Leonard Cohen, Henry Miller, Sol Yurick, Norman Mailer, Ralph Ellison, Dick Higgins, Wolf Vostell, John Cage, Rex Reed, Carl Schorske, Herbert Marcuse, and many other distinguished figures from the overground and underground 1960s intellectual scene.

Fluxus events found a home on the pages of *Books,* and Something Else Press was a frequent advertiser, so the presence of Higgins, Vostell, and Cage on the list of contributors is no accident. Even if *Books* was the creation of an uptown ad man, the downtown connections were more than circumstantial. **Agel's notion of "happening" merged the everyday pop culture, street sense of the word with a sensibility for nonlinear, participatory, intermedia models of performance.** The result was an eclectic monthly that combined a kaleidoscopic approach to editorial content with a deliberately homemade cut-and-paste graphic style worthy of a radical rag with the sort of intellectual horizons associated with the highbrow world and wit of Agel's weekly of choice: the *New Yorker.* Every issue featured "The Cocktail Party," Agel's carousel of publishing news and literary gossip modeled after the *New Yorker*'s "Talk of the Town."[18] The overall mix was unpredictable: doodles, satirical cartoons, hand-drawn titles, photo collages, galaxies of puns, banner headlines excerpted from the writings of thinkers on the left but also on the right (viz., Herman Kahn), patchwork quilts of quotations, ads for xerography as a way to transform everyman into a publisher. There were frequent calls for reader submissions on topics like "the book that shook me up" or "a book is...," with the results routinely published, and reader-initiated pieces like a February 1967 column listing the music preferences of four random Eastchester, New York, teens. *Books* even hosted one of the earliest public presentations of Ted Nelson's hypertextual environment, Project Xanadu.[19] Summaries of hundreds of new publications anchored the back pages of every issue.

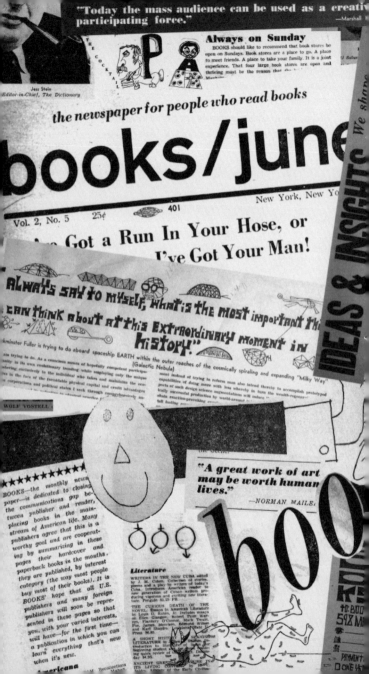

UNCLE NORMAN MAKES THE OB-SCEN

Oh, Yes, This Is The Cocktail Party

"One m... lives, then the inqu... into a shell and is cracked by fourteen aesthetic impulse."

On going back to his conventional prose style:

Robert L. Bernstein
President, Bowdoin House

SIR: My check for a two-year re-subscription is enclosed, but I'd appreciate having more book news and less about LSD and related subjects and other somewhat pointless articles.

EMILY NOBLE
New York, N.Y.

You Are _____ tant Person

Sociology

JAPANESE YOUTH CONFRONTS RELIGION: A Sociological Survey by Fernando M. Masabe. Analysis of what young Japanese people think of God, by a professor of social psychology at Sophia University. Tokyo. Tuttle $6.00.

MERCHANTS OF LABOR: The Mexi-_____ bracero Story by Ernesto Galarza. _____ migration of Mexican _____ social document, read-_____ Nally & Loftin

New New New New

_____ Blanche Knopf with their original and only bartoi 40 years ago. _____ dog was not a good house pet, and the Knopfs never had another.

By Saul Bellow

BROTHERS OF UTERICA by Benjamin Capps. Group of idealists attempt _____ found a Utopian community in the _____ rican Southwest in 1850. Mere-_____ Press $5.95.

_____YS IN OUR HANDS by Helen _____ Wallace. Constructive proj-

By Ralph Elli_____

Sensesorship

Information Explosion Challenges Book Publishing

What wo_____
What was i_____
What was the bo_____
_____lightened you, go_____
_____lightened you, got you a_____
_____lightened you, got you any
changed your life? Send_____
changed your life_____
changed_____

_____ience. BOOKS pays_
your experience. BOOKS pays
for each account used. (No manuscri
for each account used. (No manuscri
for each account used. (No manuscri
can be returned.) BOOKS, 598 Madis
_____med.) BOOKS, 598 Madi_

CocktalePartyCocktalePartyCocktalePartyCocktaleP

Three clips from new Robert ("Pull My Daisy") Frank's film, originally based on "Kaddish," Allen Ginsberg's poem. Film fea-tures Julius Orlovsky, patient at Central Islip State Hospital and brother of long-time Ginsberg friend Peter Orlovsky. Frank told BOOKS, "Julius played himself in the first part of the film, then disappeared. We had to get an actor to play him. Part of the film is my view of New York. Sam Shephard wrote certain scenes, but I made up most of it as I _____ editing the film now. It should be ready in two months. Allen _____ reluctantly gave up star billing."

Cocktail Party
(continued from _____)

the terrific torontian
The Medium Is the Massage was born on the pages
of *Books*.

— born in the anecdotal sense that the project was a
direct outcome of Agel's editorial work...
— born in the general sense that the success of *Books*
had cemented Agel's understanding of himself not
as a *book packager* but as **a book producer operating like a theatrical or cinematographic producer**:
hiring talent, developing a concept, shaping the
script, putting together the deal, overseeing the final
cut, and devising a distribution strategy...[20]
— born in the stylistic sense, inasmuch as the rapid-
fire, verbal-visual quotation/collage had become a
Books trademark (though in a graphically slapdash
manner that Fiore would interpret and raise to a new
level of graphic refinement)...
— born in the promotional sense, given that the book's
transformation into a cultural *happening* was the
outcome of an elaborate campaign launched on the
pages of *Books*.

Contrary to what Agel was wont to claim, he did
not "discover" McLuhan in the wake of the May 26, 1964,
publication of *Understanding Media*. If that honor goes
to anyone, it goes to Gerald Feigen and Howard Gossage,
the former a doctor and the latter a California advertising
executive, who (with help from Tom Wolfe) brought the
University of Toronto English professor to New York City
in May 1965 to launch his career as a celebrity.[21] What Agel
did "discover" in McLuhan's work (and in this he may have
been aided by Fiore) was **an opening toward electronic
and television age models of communication** like the
ones that McLuhan had analyzed critically for decades but
was now beginning to put into practice.

I'M TOUGH

The crafty cubist J I v E of the daily
press awakening the political appetite of
COSMIC MAN

McLuhan's experiments to date with nonstandard print formats had been limited to the modest dialogue between ads and text staged in *The Mechanical Bride* (1951) and the futurist/vorticist vein of typographical experimentation found in the mimeographed *Counterblast* (1954) and *Verbi-Voco-Visual Explorations* (1957).[22] The mosaic mode of exposition tested out in *The Gutenberg Galaxy* (1962), where sloganlike headings frame a succession of one-hundred-plus three-to-five-page minichapter units, was rather more academic, intended to derail linear models of historiography and to honor "a mosaic of perpetually interacting forms that have undergone kaleidoscopic transformation."[23] It remained conventional enough to offend detractors mostly within the scholarly community.

The situation shifted by the time of McLuhan and Agel's initial contacts. From the start, their exchanges hinge on **the use of pictorial materials to engage younger audiences**. On June 4, 1965, Agel writes about a "profusely illustrated" article that he is preparing on McLuhan's work and closes with a question: "Do you believe that a children's book could be developed from *Understanding Media*? **I LOVE YOUR PUNS.**"[24] McLuhan replies, mentioning a possible young people's guide to media built on clippings from magazines.[25] A dinner in New York City follows with Agel in the company of his next-door neighbor at 598 Madison Avenue, Fiore. The idea for the pairing may have been Fiore's own: "I generated it to the extent that I talked with Agel and suggested that maybe McLuhan and I could [collaborate], because I had some idea[s]."[26] Two months later both are "anxious to show [McLuhan] our illustrated mock-up of a book that we are developing based on your published works and per our talk that night at dinner. We don't want to put it into final shape until you have seen and approved *our technique*."[27]

The McLuhan Galaxy

By dawn's early light a young couple neck on Avenue A in New York's low-er East Side. In her left hand she holds a paperback copy of "Understanding Media."

In a poetry class in Greenwich Village's New School, the book that really grabbed students this summer was an all-prose work, "Understanding Media."

On the West Coast, in a converted firehouse that serves as the office of San Francisco's most far-out, most-talked-about, perhaps most effective advertising agency, Jessica Mitford, Herbert Gold, Tom Wolfe and stars from the firmaments of design, theatre, advertising, and journalism gath-

(continued on following page)

"The problem is not that Johnny can't read, but that in an age of depth involvement Johnny can't visualize distant goals. If any entire year college program were spent in understanding the phrase 'the very silence,' the world might soon have an adequate supply of competent minds. We must awaken perception. Education should move toward discovery and away from instruction."

"Generals always prepare for the last war. If it works, it's obsolete. Ads are by far the best part of any magazine or newspaper."

"If the Voice of America suddenly switched to jazz, the Kremlin would have reason to crumble. It would be almost as effective as if the Russian citizens had copies of Sears, Roebuck catalogues to goggle at, instead of our dreary propaganda for the American way of life. In Houston's Astrodome the audience is more involved in a baseball game than it is out-of-doors, because its senses are extended technologically by electricity; the audience participates."

"The poverty of the middle is its psychic blight. Providing modes of thought, a TV cut makes the middle class and departmental executive job of the ironies of Western man that he has never felt any about invention as a thrust way of life."

"The cold war is largely a conflict between cultures where different sense priorities prevail. The U.S. is eye-oriented. The Soviet Union, with its limited tradition of literacy, is ear-oriented. This is why the Russians reacted so violently to the visual espionage of the American U-2 spy fly, and why Americans reacted so violently to electronic eavesdropping in the Moscow embassy. Each regards the other's method as an atrocious violation of privacy. We'll go right on banging our heads into a wall until we realize that these basic differences in approach exist."

A foretaste of the technique in question can be found in the September 1965 issue of *Books*, the front page of which led with "The McLuhan Galaxy," a montage of cartoons and quotations radiating outward from a book-slaying, television-antenna-crowned McLuhan. It was accompanied by a lengthy "interview" that hails *Understanding Media* as the "'must read' book in the country today" and implements what will later become the method of the McLuhan/Agel/Fiore inventorying of media effects: a sequence of quotations fired one after the other, interrupted only by questions—"why is everyone reading field Marshall McLuhan?" "what the hell *is* going on?" "**OK, WHAT'S THE MESSAGE?**"—and designed to swarm the reader with information. In the interview's midst, Agel dutifully inserts McLuhan's call for the "fresh air reeducation of book culture."

By the end of the year a contract has been drafted "to prepare for your [McLuhan's] co-authorship (*we'll be doing all the work; you'll be approving*) of a book based on *Media* and *Gutenberg*."[28] The final document, dated February 19, 1966, and preserved in the McLuhan archives in Ottawa, is telling as regards the genesis of the still-untitled book. The main paragraph reads:

> You agree to have MARSHALL McLUHAN as President of McLuhan Associates, Ltd. collaborate with QUENTIN FIORE (Fiore) in the preparation of a manuscript and illustrations of the Work for THE AGEL PUBLISHING CO., INC. (Agel). Fiore will be responsible for the mechanicals for camera. The manuscript shall consist of approximately 30,000 to 50,000 words including an introductory essay of approximately 10,000 to 12,000 words; approximately 100 illustrative spreads containing 100 to 150 illustrations, captions and running text; front and back matter; design and illustrations of covers I and IV, all of which will constitute the basic presentation of McLuhan's ideas on media and communication.[29]

The contract grants full ownership to Agel, publication rights to Bantam Books, equal billing to Fiore and McLuhan as authors, and the listing "co-ordinated by" to the Agel Publishing Company. Though the details of what transpired during the backstage negotiations in late 1965 remain unknown, it appears that, despite McLuhan's newfound prominence, the project was turned down by well over a dozen publishers before the Bantam deal was signed.[30] Skeptical of the book's mass appeal, Bantam placed restrictions on the production budget and fixed the initial print run at thirty-five thousand copies: small for a mass-market paperback, large for a work of an experimental nature.

Little does it matter. Agel was confident in the success of the newfound formula (even if the slight discrepancies between the above description and *The Medium Is the Massage*—the absence of an introduction, for instance— still suggest a certain fluidity). So confident that, even *before* signing the Bantam contract, he was lining up a series. In early January 1966 he wrote to R. Buckminster Fuller with a proposal nearly identical to the one offered to McLuhan. Fuller replied in the affirmative: "I would be delighted to have you make a comprehensive contraction of my writing, for young people, to be published in a book to be produced by your office."[31] Several years would pass before the agreement would bear fruit in the form of the INVENTORY BOOK that is perhaps Fiore/Agel's graphic masterpiece: *I Seem to Be a Verb.*

The launch of the series went public with the publication in the March 1966 issue of *Books* of an article titled "McLuhan, Fiore Write on Restructured Man":

In late February the Terrific Torontian contracted for Book Number Five—a paperback original that he'll co-author with Quentin Fiore for publication this summer by Bantam Books. Mr. Fiore, of New York, is typographic man *par excellence*—a graphics designer specializing in scholarly books and materials for foundations. He is design consultant to the Ford Foundation. Every American comes into contact an average of 10 times a day with one of Mr. Fiore's greatest design achievements: The alphabet that appears on the telephone dial. The McLuhan-Fiore book extends their insights into media and communication. It will demonstrate how deeply the new electric technology has restructured man's thoughts, feelings and actions—his *everyday life*, commenting upon some of the consequences of these new perceptions and actions. **Heavily illustrated.**

A contract for the next INVENTORY BOOK, initially titled *The Effects of Automation* but later published as *War and Peace in the Global Village*, was signed by the end of 1966. Another dozen projects were somewhere in the pipeline at Agel Publishing by decade's end.

the (children's) book of the year

The March 1966 issue of *Books* didn't just announce a new work by the Terrific Torontian. It also inaugurated a novel press campaign that would unfold over the next two years, eventually spilling over onto the pages of the *New York Times*. Long before Book Number Five had a working title, let alone existed in draft form, the marketing tools of the movie industry were mobilized to build a market.

A mysterious ad appeared on page 7, beneath "The Cocktail Party":

Coming Soon:

A book that will show what's happening when what's happening is happening. It predicts the present. Two clues: "The thing of it is," Montaigne said, "that we must live with the living." And, "The songs made me," Goethe said, "not I them."

It's The Book of the Year.
Watch this space for details.

In April 1966 the message became **Coming Nearer** and was driven home by ever more frequent attention to McLuhan. By May the self-designated Book of the Year was **Coming Even Nearer**. By July the book had a title.[32] By August the refrain of —**yes, "the Massage"**, destined to become the book's lead-page layout, had become integral to the press campaign. Soon it was accompanied by provocations of a different sort: ones framed by the theme of informational friction as instantiated by crossed female legs laced up in fishnet stockings, by slogans like "The Eyes Had It, Now For The Ears," by prone portrayals of McLuhan himself as if on a psychiatric couch. An admirer of Alfred Hitchcock, Agel couldn't resist the temptation to indulge in an occasional insider's joke. The January 1967 ad that asked "who slams the door of technological awareness in his face?" was built around the photograph of an anonymous youth: the very same youth who appears on page 17 of *The Medium Is the Massage* across from the title "**your neighborhood**." That awareness-deprived youth is none other than Agel himself, pictured three decades earlier in a photo plucked from a family album.

When the book was released in March 1967, half a year late and one year into the advertising campaign, Agel shifted gears. He lined up a television special titled *This Is Marshall McLuhan: The Medium Is the Massage*, part of NBC's legendary *Experiment in Television* series, which ran on March 19 and included props like a ball of dough being massaged by the guest of honor as he evoked massages of a more figurative nature. Agel also published ads in the *New York Times* in the form of a quiz, titled "Are you getting the massage?" based on some of the very questions formulated as the structural grid for *The Medium Is the Massage*:

> Why is **art** anything you can get away with?
> Why is today's **child** growing up absurd?

Why is a new form of **politics** emerging?

Why is it the **business** of the future to be dangerous?

Why is our claim to **privacy** seriously threatened?

Why do some like it **hot**, some like it **cold**?

He also ran a long stream of mini-advertisements in *Books* that leveraged the polemics triggered by the book as summons to its readers to "decide for themselves." (A year later the same tactic was repeated in promoting *War and Peace in the Global Village* through the scattershot publication of so-called "Insights" throughout the print media.)

Decide for Yourself:

"With all the zeal of a convert, I would like to urge everybody not to buy this book . . ."
—*The New York Times Book Review.*

"Book Called Literary LSD Trip."
—*Headline, Newark Evening News.*

Decide for yourself: Read "The Medium is the Massage," by Marshall McLuhan and Quentin Fiore, $10.95 **Random House hardcover edition. $1.45 Bantam Books paperback.**

Agel's final move came during the spring as the book was beginning to clamber its way to the top of national best-seller lists. The May issue of *Books* published a full-page interview with yet another figure with a comprehensive approach to the role of producer: John Simon, head of the Popular Artists and Repertoire division at Columbia Records. ("The A & R producer is like the director *and* producer in a movie or play," opines Simon, before going on to assert that "an editor should be interested in all book processes, including advertising. As for the future of the book business...it wouldn't surprise me if data machines start shaping stories.")[33] Two months later, *The Medium Is the Massage with Marshall McLuhan,* **The First Spoken Arts Record You Can Dance To**, was issued by Columbia Records, with Simon as producer, McLuhan, Fiore, and Agel as authors, and Agel listed as having "conceived and coordinated" everything.[34] In the letter that sought McLuhan's approval for the project, Agel's pitch was that the LP is

to be "designed for young people—it is designed to be a 40-minute interface—it is designed to be heard again and again and again and again and again, like a pop record."[35] A forty-minute interface for *The Gutenberg Galaxy* was planned as an encore performance, but the University of Toronto Press was not about to take any chances with its star performer. **What part of NO don't you understand, Mr. Agel?**

Unlike McLuhan's recorded Dew Line Platter-tudes, which remained little more than private pranks, the Columbia record was distributed like a conventional LP. It was promoted by Agel through both traditional means, such as radio broadcasts, and novel ones, such as mock street protests by placard-carrying "mini-skirted misses parading around the advertising districts in New York, Los Angeles, San Francisco, Chicago and Boston." The pop McLuhan game was now so public that even the *New York Times*' stringers wanted a piece of the action. "This Time the Medium Is the Mini" read the title of their reportage, accompanied by a photo captioned "Medium employed is a non-tribal placard."[36]

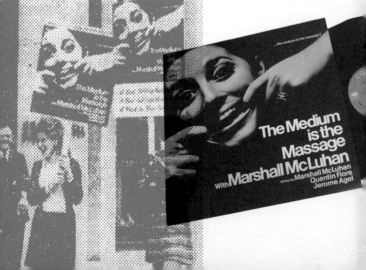

Marshall McLuhan
Author of UNDERSTANDING MEDIA

Quentin Fiore

The Medium
is the Massage

An Inventory of Effects

R3348 ★ $1.45 ★ A BANTAM BOOK

ook

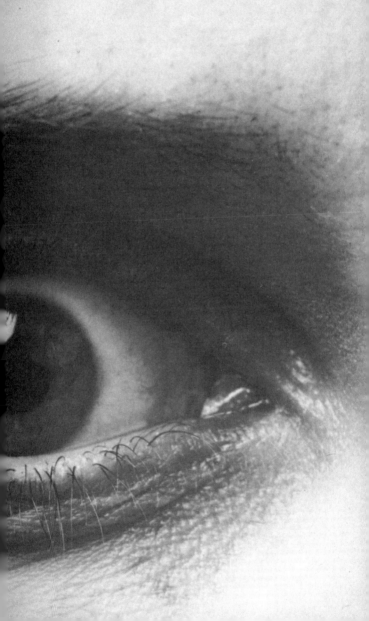

of the eye...

"Authorship"—in the sense we know it today, individual intellectual effort related to the book as an economic commodity—was practically unknown before the advent of print technology. Medieval scholars were indifferent to the precise identity of the "books" they studied. In turn, they rarely signed even what was clearly their own. They were a humble service organization. Procuring texts was often a very tedious and time-consuming task. Many small texts were transmitted into volumes of miscellaneous content, very much like "jottings" in a scrapbook, and, in this transmission, authorship was often lost.

The invention of printing did away with anonymity, fostering ideas of literary fame and the habit of considering intellectual effort as private property. Mechanical multiples of the same text created a public—a reading public. The rising consumer-oriented culture became concerned with labels of authenticity and protection against theft and piracy. The idea of copyright—"the exclusive right to reproduce, publish, and sell the matter and form of a literary or artistic work"—was born.

Xerography—every man's brain-picker—heralds the times of instant publishing. Anybody can now become both author and publisher. Take any books on any subject and custom-make your own book by simply xeroxing a chapter from this one, a chapter from that one—instant steal!

As new technologies come into play, people are less and less convinced of the importance of self-expression. Teamwork succeeds private effort.

A ditto, ditto device.
"   "   "   "

A ditto, ditto device.
"   "   "   "

A ditto, ditto device.
"   "   "   "

the e/a switch

The external history of the shaping of *The Medium Is the Massage* as a publishing event has embedded within it an internal history in which are nested two overlapping questions: the role of Fiore as designer/coauthor and the issue of just how the design and drafting process unfolded. At some point along this inside track, someone flipped the switch that turned *message* into *massage*, transforming the professorial one-man act of the author of *Understanding Media* into a McLuhan/Agel/Fiore triple threat.

According to Eric McLuhan, that switch was thrown not by design but by error. *Massage* was a typo, welcomed in the Joycean manner: "When McLuhan saw the typo he exclaimed, 'Leave it alone! It's great and right on target!' Now there are four possible readings for the last word of the title, all of them accurate:

> **Message** and
> **Mess Age,**
> **Massage** and
> **Mass Age**."[37]

McLuhan's biographers omit the tale of the typo. W. Terrence Gordon surmises that "by the time [the book] appeared in 1967, McLuhan no doubt recognized that his original saying had become a cliché and welcomed the opportunity to throw it back on the compost heap of language to recycle and revitalize it."[38] Philippe Marchand seems to concur, dating the shift to a May 1966 presentation at the Laurentian management conference where McLuhan led off a salvo of aphorisms with the oracular pronouncement: "No longer will I say that the medium is the message. I've changed my thinking…. From now on, I believe that the medium is the *massage*."[39] The switch is repeated in a public lecture given at the Kaufmann Art Gallery in New York City on May 7. Whatever the case may be, May 1966 still situates the switch well within the book's development timeline. This would have been months into the ad campaign and nearly a year after Agel/Fiore presented the first illustrated mock-up of their technique, which means that there was plenty of time for an early mechanical to contain the felicitous *e*-to-*a* swerve, whether intentional or unintentional.

Little does it matter: the turn from *message* to *massage* was more than a public relations gambit or an addition to the already extensive catalog of McLuhan puns. It signals two broader shifts. The first is in McLuhan's thought, from his prior insistence on the environment as "extension" to the more forceful concept of the "total media work-over." The second is in his language, from linear modes of exposition to "a sort of post-alphabetic, non-syntactical language more appropriate to a vision which trumpets the end of the Gutenberg era."[40] Fiore's role in shaping the second is usually acknowledged in passing by all but design historians, with McLuhan treated as the book's de facto author. Agel's role is passed over in silence or embarrassment. After all, what is a book *coordinator*? The reviewers were puzzled.

The shortcut is understandable given that the ideas (though not always the textual materials) are indeed McLuhan's and that, however decisive were the roles performed by coordinator and coauthor, *The Medium Is the Massage* has become an enduring entry point to McLuhan's (not Fiore's or Agel's) thought: "the best explication yet of Beginning McLuhanism," writes Fremont-Smith; "McLuhan made easy," in Marchand's words.[41] Yet if Agel is responsible for the book's overall concept and contours, it was mostly Fiore who wrestled with the professor's (sometimes clotted) prose, who collected and culled the visual materials, and who transfigured Agel's slapdash graphic ideas into a pop typophotographic synthesis of the first order.

Fiore brought to his coauthorial responsibilities a successful career as a New York–based graphic design and telecommunications consultant who had worked for leading foundations (Ford), companies (Christian Dior, Bonwit Teller), and research centers (Bell Labs). He had done design work for a wide array of publications, from commercial magazines (*McCall's*, *Life*) to the University of Michigan Press (for whom he designed books on surrealism and leftist politics) to *Crawdaddy*, the first rock magazine (to which he contributed a cover featuring the Kinks) to George Braziller (for whom he designed Gyorgy Kepes's important Vision + Value series).[42] In addition to directing some industrial training films for Bell Labs and commercials for Gulf & Western, Fiore was actively involved in developing Homefax at NBC/RCA: a television-based facsimile system and forerunner of videotext systems, in connection with which he was entrusted with the design of one of several electronically distributed newspapers. Until the time that *The Medium Is the Massage* brought him international fame, Fiore's most visible creation was, as noted earlier, the alphabet on the rotary dial of the standard Bell telephone designed by Henry Dreyfuss.

This interest in electronic technologies was uniquely paired, in Fiore's case, with a devotion to **the history of lettering, from calligraphy to electronic typography**. Self-trained as a designer, Fiore had studied painting with George Grosz and Hans Hofmann, done a brief stint with Moholy-Nagy at the Chicago Bauhaus, and then landed in New York, where he worked as a lettering artist for Lester Beall, one of the leading modernist graphic designers on this side of the Atlantic. During subsequent years, he became an avid student of **ILLUMINATED MANUSCRIPTS** and of the history of typography and papermaking, contributing a technical study on the handmanufacture of paper to the review *Industrial Design*.[43] (He devoted most of the 1980s to another abiding passion:

designing leather-bound, illustrated editions of classical and Renaissance masterpieces for the Franklin Library.)[44] In short, dubbing Fiore a "typographic man par excellence" in the March 1966 issue of *Books*, Agel was doing more than casting his collaborator in a convenient *Gutenberg Galaxy* mold. He was calling attention to the ideal character of the pairing of McLuhan with a designer-double who combined an eclectic, experimental sensibility, open to contemporary informatics and pop culture, with in-depth knowledge about the history of lettering and the print and preprint past.

the ears have it

While there is no disputing Agel's central role as coordinator of the triangular collaboration that gave rise to *The Medium Is the Massage*, there is less agreement about the book's gestation. In a letter dated December 1, 1966, McLuhan found himself reassuring McGraw-Hill that the Agel book wouldn't compete with *Understanding Media*. "I didn't write anything for that book," he protested. "It is excerpts with pictures."[45] According to this scenario, McLuhan's role was limited to serving as the "adviser and approver" of an illustrated book entirely based on his prior published works and in which he had a minor hand.[46] Marchand asserts that McLuhan "changed only one word"; all the rest was done by Fiore and Agel.[47] A review of the McLuhan Archives at the Canadian national library in Ottawa only partly confirms this scenario, devised defensively to fend off objections from other publishers.

In point of fact, McLuhan did quite a bit more than simply approve the overall concept and sign off on the mechanicals. There were several lengthy face-to-face conversations about the book, and he "scrutinized every spread" at various stages: from the initial packet delivered by Agel and Fiore in May 1966—"a title page, telegraphic one-liners (one to a page), and the opening essay...[plus] following the opening text will be the chunk of illustrations, to be followed by the captions and the credits"—to the final layout.[48] He also carefully pored over the final typescript provided by Agel and Fiore, making numerous sentence-long additions and corrections, as well as altering its phraseology. Some examples:

— on page 9, McLuhan changed the phrase "Wars, revolutions, civil uprisings are interactions made possible by the electric informational media" to "Wars, revolutions, civil uprisings are interfaces within the new environments created by electric informational media"; the passage was to appear on the middle of page 10, but was moved forward during a later edit, most likely by Agel.

— on page 10, McLuhan altered the phrase "Our time is a time for crossing new barriers, for erasing old categories, for sniffing around" to "Our time is a time for crossing barriers, for erasing old categories, for probing around"; in a subsequent edit, Agel apparently substituted "probing around" with "probing ground."

— on page 18, the final phrase, "Mere instruction will not suffice," is a McLuhan add-on; the point is central to a number of his post–*Understanding Media* pronouncements on the reform of education.

— on page 69, McLuhan completed the phrase "the technique of suspended judgment" with "is the discovery of the twentieth century as the technique of invention is the discovery of the nineteenth"; the sentence merges the thoughts of Bertrand Russell and Alfred North Whitehead, rephrasing a longer passage from *Understanding Media* (p. 63).

— on page 123, McLuhan adds to a page devoted to exploring the effects of xerography the sentence "Teamwork succeeds private effort," paraphrasing one of *Understanding Media*'s recurring themes.

— on page 137, the quote "I wouldn't be seen dead with a living work of art" attributed to a "museum curator" is yet another late McLuhan addition; the anecdote postdates *Understanding Media*.

As indicated, some of these adjustments are self-quotations or paraphrases. Others are updatings, meant to bring the book closer to McLuhan's thought circa 1966. Though nontrivial in nature, none substantially alters a text that, in effect, hinges on reworkings of passages from *Understanding Media* and *The Gutenberg Galaxy*, as well as subsequent writings—the latter representing one of the collators' main sources.[49]

This said, **The Medium Is the Massage cannot be described as a book "by Marshall McLuhan" in any simple sense.** Fiore's account may be taken as authoritative:

> There was no special, "original," manuscript for the book. The idea was to select Marshall McLuhan's views from previous publications, heavily editing them, and presenting them in isolated "patches" i.e., individual pages of doublespreads with appropriate accompanying art work, all with a view towards **producing a more appealing presentation which would be accessible to a wide public.**[50]

The result is that most of the text has no exact counterpart elsewhere. The graphic textures within which the text is woven are entirely the work of Agel and Fiore. None of the visuals was suggested by or traceable to McLuhan, with four exceptions.

Three of these exceptions derive from the work of Lewis Carroll, pointed to approvingly in *Understanding Media* because, in *Alice in Wonderland*, "times and spaces are neither uniform nor continuous, as they had seemed to be since the arrival of Renaissance perspective."[51] Carroll was a McLuhan favorite, so, at first glance, they could be categorized as mere illustrations. But they are not entirely so. Fiore and Agel pick from two different editions: the 1965 University Microfilms version of the original autograph color manuscript of *Alice's Adventures under Ground* and the familiar print edition (1866) of *Alice's Adventures in Wonderland* with etchings by John Tenniel. A fragment from the first that pits Alice against the Queen in a battle over whether the study of evidence precedes the making of judgments is reproduced in black and white on pages **42–43** in order to set up a restatement of McLuhan's familiar argument about the determining role

played by alphabetic writing in establishing linearity as an organizing principle of life on pages 44–45.

Why was the microfilm facsimile selected when the standard print edition appears in the later portions of the book (pp. 141–42, 153)? The likely answer is found on the front cover of the October 1965 issue of *Books,* which hails the microfilm as a major publishing event:

> "Now I can do no more—what will become of me?" said Alice after eating a mushroom that made her grow larger and larger. Also growing larger and larger—with the end indeterminate—is University Microfilms' "entirely new plan in book publishing" to reproduce and publish book-size facsimiles of original manuscripts and drawings for libraries and book buyers. Just published: a facsimile of Lewis Carroll's original hand-written and illustrated *Alice's Adventures Underground.* University Microfilms, based in Ann Arbor, is a subsidiary of Xerox. "Anything the eye can see..."[52]

McLuhan had said similar things in a review published the very same month in the *New York Herald Tribune*'s *Book Week* and would use the juxtaposition of facsimile with published edition in his 1968 collaboration with Harley Parker, *Through the Vanishing Point.* A coincidence? Surely not. But it's hard to establish whether the instigator was McLuhan. What is certain is that, as a key mid-1960s McLuhan theme, **XEROGRAPHY** will be featured on page 123 of *The Medium Is the Massage,* holding forth the promise of instant self-publishing (not to mention instant literary theft) and calling into question the survival of the institution of authorship. So, however subtly, the visual quotation of the Carroll microfilm on pages 42–43 points forward within the text. When placed in dialogue with the subsequent recourse to the print edition, it also contributes to the setting up of a larger equation between the notion of Carroll as a post-Euclidean, nonlinear thinker and a new media constellation in which the gap once separating handwritten manuscripts from print artifacts from television-age publishing models has collapsed. The equation may be McLuhan's, but it is also one that directly reflects Agel's and Fiore's own commitments to **experimenting with new communicational models**.

The sole instance of a direct visual borrowing from McLuhan must again be characterized not as a simple quotation or illustration but as an *interpretive* intervention on the part of the coauthor and coordinator. On page 121, right before the copyright and xerography discussion alluded to above, another visual echo occurs: a full-page reprise of a trick student photograph from Moholy-Nagy's *Vision in Motion* that McLuhan had placed alongside the title

page of *Verbi-Voco-Visual Explorations*.[53] Moholy-Nagy's caption motivated McLuhan's choice: it reads, "Can you see with your ear? Can you hear with your eye?" The photograph was a demonstration of the use of prisms for shifting details in objects, so the ear hovers, ghostlike and unattached, over an artificially darkened male eye socket. Fiore and Agel had the image reshot by Peter Moore, the noted photographer of multimedia happenings, Fluxus events, and performance art. It was then reworked as a photomontage such that the ear appears directly *sutured* onto the male model's face, literalizing the description on the subsequent page of television's new sensorium with its *omnipresent ear* and *moving eye*. Here McLuhan's mantra that *media are extensions of the human body* is translated into one of the book's most compelling graphic composites.

over easy

I have lingered over the above minutiae because they hint at one of the defining attributes of the verbal-visual texture of *The Medium Is the Massage*: its high degree of self-reflexivity. This characteristic comes into sharper focus when one turns to an examination of the volume's overall contours, from the opening Good Morning! to the concluding view of earth from the moon sent back by NASA's Lunar Orbiter 1—its tacit Good Night! The pairing is mirrored by another symmetrical framing device: an initial sounding the drumbeat of total change with respect to you, your life, and your world, matched by a valedictory posing of the question "who are you?"

The fit between opening and closing is no accident in a book built on local verbal-visual suites—"patches," as Fiore calls them—slotted into broader structures of meaning. "In designing the *Massage* book," Fiore averred, "I wanted to avoid the 'lineality' of the standard book, and create...*iconic* double-spreads, each expressing a particular point MM was dealing with in his other books."[54] (To this end, the paperback original, which employed a printing process "never before used for mass-market paperback production," had a perfect binding—the cover is glued to the side of the spine—thereby minimizing the gutter and permitting the book to sit flat.)[55] A case in point is the introductory crescendo (pp. 1–25), devised as one of five chapterlike units. So much is served up so compactly here, thanks to the interplay between Fiore's design efforts and Agel's editorial handiwork, that the following commentary on the sequencing of "iconic double-spreads" only begins to tell the full story.

FRAME 1

Blank inside cover on the left; on the right, a cheery breakfast greeting is paired with the photograph of a logo printed on a raw egg yolk through a no-pressure, no-contact printing technique developed by the Electrostatic Printing Corporation of America (EPC). The photograph is the first of the repurposed press clippings with a covert McLuhan tie-in scattered throughout *The Medium Is the Massage*. Its source is a *Newsweek* science special report, dated January 24, 1966, and here, just as in its original context, the printed egg looms as an enigma at the beginning of the text. The *Newsweek* caption read, "Electrostatic egg: Message of consuming interest," leading into an article titled "Good-by to Gutenberg" that begins with McLuhan's claim that newspapers and books will soon cease to exist. The accent now falls not on adieus and deaths ("Good-by") but on awakenings ("Good Morning!"), with the reader/eater invited to sit down, take his or her seat at a post-Gutenbergian symposium, and WAKE UP. The printed egg becomes less an icon of print culture's demise than of the new tactility and freedoms that characterize the electronic age: television that tattoos its message directly on our skins, cool media that demand completion through haptic audience participation, an unembarrassed embrace of nudity and new sexual freedoms. The message of consuming interest is that a new day has begun.

FRAME 3

Another turn of the page and the reader grapples with the perplexity provoked by the *message* to *massage* switch in the title: the *e/a* switch around which Agel built his advertising campaign ...the massage? (instead of the more familiar McLuhan message): how so? Another self-reference may be buried here: it is Fiore who appears to be cast in the role of the perplexed reader/listener; Fiore who, as noted below, once described *The Medium Is the Massage* as *A Guide for the Perplexed*, recalling Maimonides's three-volume letter to his student, Joseph ben Judah.[56]

FRAME 2

The reader flips the page to meet both title and colophon, printed vertically in white against the grainy backdrop of a celebrated *Time-Life* photograph: a high-speed exposure, shot on January 1, 1948, of the facial distortions endured by a volunteer in a 300 mph wind bailout experiment conducted by the U.S. Navy—the third in a sequence that shows the gradual transformation of an ordinary face into a twisted mask. This reshaping of humankind's face because of wind acceleration— read *the rate of technological change, the pace of everyday life, information overload*—is echoed at the book's conclusion where the mutable nature of contemporary identity will be figured instead by three pages (pp. 152, 154–55) filled with blank numbered faces, all available as provisional answers to the question of *Who are you?* Here, as elsewhere, literalization is one of Fiore's key design strategies. The photograph somatizes McLuhan's notion that informational speed remolds the human psyche just as an ear sutured onto the face somatizes the notion of media as prostheses.

FRAME 4

The banner headline "AND HOW!" stretches across the top, butting up against the right margin. Under it appears quote #1 from Alfred North Whitehead's *Symbolism: Its Meaning and Effect* (1927), concerning the wreckage inflicted on civilizations over human history by major advances. The thread will be picked up again on page 10 in the form of a second Whitehead quote, this time from *Adventures in Ideas* (1933). Both prefigure the final sentence of *The Medium Is the Massage*, drawn from the final paragraph of *Science and the Modern World* (1925): "It is the business of the future to be dangerous." The accompanying image of the setting earth—not the setting sun—as seen from Orbiter 1 drives home the inversion in perspective the book as a whole sets out to promote: a turn away from the wreckage of the past toward future challenges; the recognition of perils but within the framework of the reassuring promise that *there is absolutely no inevitability as long as there is a willingness to contemplate what is happening* (p. 25).

FRAME 5

The reader turns the page to encounter the book's prologue, where the cupped masculine hand of the perplexed reader/listener on pages 4–5 is displaced by text on the left and a graceful female wrist and extended hand showing off a wedding ring against a white background on the right. The photograph has been removed from its original context, a September 1956 ad campaign for Artcarved diamond and wedding rings, in which it appeared flanked by the question: "Which ring can you be sure will always keep its value?" Fiore positions it right where the text asserts that ours is an "Age of Anxiety," redoubling the anxiety through the unlikely caption: "30-million toy trucks were bought in the U.S. in 1966." An explanation arrives on the following page: "When two seemingly disparate elements are imaginatively poised, put in apposition in new and unique ways, startling discoveries often result." What do toys for mechanical brides have in common with toys for mechanically inclined boys? Does a toy truck = a wedding ring, since both are vehicles of desire? How can we be sure that such a vehicle will retain its value or uniqueness in the Mass Age?

FRAME 7

Next comes the first barrage of addresses to the reader: "How much do you make? Have you ever contemplated suicide? Are you now or have you ever been...?" The passage is titled "you" and is juxtaposed with the motif of concentric circles that fills the right page. The notion of concentricity, of outward and inward movement back and forth between *you <> family <> government <> society <> the world* structures the whole of pages 12–24. Here Fiore graphically transcribes a leitmotif from *Understanding Media*:

> It is a redundant form inevitable to the electric age, in which the concentric pattern is imposed by the instant quality, and overlay in depth, of electric speed. But the concentric with its endless intersection of planes is necessary for insight. In fact, it is the technique of insight, and as such is necessary for media study, since no medium has its meaning or existence alone, but only in constant interplay with other media.[57]

The redundancy assumes the form of an image first presented full page that is repeated and reframed as a thumbnail on the successive page. Similar patterns of repetition with differences, much like the Vichian *ricorsi* that McLuhan frequently invoked, will mark the text's unfolding from beginning to end.

FRAME 6

We flip the page only to find that the hand has been rotated and brought uncomfortably close: so close that it appears reduced to a single giant fingerprint—the juridical signature of the self in the Mass Age, but also a map of concentric flows and patterns. The direct imprint of the body, the fingerprint anticipates the you on page 12 with its concentric circles.

FRAMES 8–12

From page 14 forward, the path from individual to society to world takes the form of a sequence of texts on the left juxtaposed with full-page icons on the right—circles, hat rack, photo album, the circuit board, a grid of noses—with the latter bouncing off the text in a para-illustrative, surrealist vein. Each anticipates the argument on the successive page, with the carryover marked by the thumbnail's presence. The object selected is significant in every case.

FRAME 8

your family, on the left; on the right, the Thonet P2204 coat rack combines bentwood construction with a lathe-turned central support (= Daddy) and s curves and hoops (= Mommy). It is a mass-produced industrial object masquerading as a sign of domesticity. Home is where you hang your coat. But has the circle so expanded, the "worldpool of information fathered by electric media" so widened that all the world's a coat rack?

FRAME 10

your education, on the left; on the right, a hybrid circuit board transports us from the mechanical world of the Thonet factory to the electric economy of today. It is a transitional circuit board, a stepping stone along the road to fully integrated chips like the one featured on pages 64–65. A ten-channel signal inverter assembly that combines elements of a printed circuit board and an integrated circuit with ten symmetrical inputs and outputs plus power and ground traces, it embodies the notion of electrical *printing,* and it serves as a graphic relay between the theme of concentricity and the notion of interconnected circuits.

FRAME 9
your neighborhood, on the left;
on the right, the photograph of
a child, presented as if slotted
into a family album. The photo is
of Agel at approximately age
eight, culled from one of his own
photo albums.[58] Agel Publishing's
next-door neighbor was the
studio of Quentin Fiore.

FRAME 11
your job, on the left; on the right,
a grid of noses forms yet another
circuit. The circuit in question is
made up of the same nose found
in the ear-eye photomontage of
page 121, here serialized in the form
of five lateral montages that have
been layered so as to yield a regular
pattern. The twentyfold nose job
gestures forward toward the
"nose counting" alluded to on page
22 and leftward (across the page)
toward the fragmentation singled
out as the defining attributes
of the old mechanical economy.
Under conditions of electric
circuitry, "specialism" and private
points of views must give way
to the realities of a Mass Age in
which work becomes pattern

recognition and individuals, no
longer reduced to the status
of statistical persons, become
a creative, participating force.

FRAME 12

your government, on the left, is
providing "yesterday's answers to
today's questions"; on the right,
Grant Wood's *American Gothic*
(1930) is making use of yesterday's
craft—forms and techniques
borrowed from sixteenth-century
Flemish models—in the service of
a backward-looking image of the
contemporary body politic. Featured
in *Time* and at Chicago's Century
of Progress World's Fair in 1933
(where inexpensive reproductions
were distributed to patrons so
that they could take home an
"authentic" midwestern souvenir),
the painting aptly communicates the
paradoxical drive to be up-to-date
and antiquated all at once. Rather
than posed, it was cobbled together
out of separate elements, featuring

Wood's own sister and dentist
dressed in nineteenth-century garb.

During this ramp-up, the prevailing message is one of
reassurance. Anxiety and perplexity are understandable responses to the crushing **ALLATONCENESS**
(or simultaneity) of the electric information age, it suggests. Because everything is changing so rapidly, so must
models of communication and cognition undergo change.
But relax! Both an advertisement and a messenger for the
Mass Age dressed up in Mass Age garb, *The Medium Is
the Massage* has the medicine for the anxious and the perplexed. Fiore explains:

> In view of the great changes that were taking place, I felt
> that utilizing humor would be the most effective way to
> reach our audience. The book was intended to be *A Guide
> for the Perplexed*. It had to convey the spirit, the "populist"
> outcry of the time in an appropriate form. The "lineality" of

FRAME 13

We flip the page and, to the left, are confronted with "the others" we have become "irrevocably involved with and responsible for," thanks to the electric information age. The husband of *American Gothic* thus makes his return as a tightly cropped solo face shot. No longer the estranged icon of a backward-looking present, he is now the familiar face of a worried neighbor or the reader's mirror image.

On the opposite page, the sequence of opening frames culminates in a column of right-aligned words. It spells out the book's key message: there is absolutely no inevitability as long as there is a willingness to contemplate what is happening. (In a 1967 interview, Agel had stated that "the message, and why it had to get out now, is on p. 25.")[59]

While not discordant with McLuhan's 1960s public pronouncements, there's a tonal shift here that appears aimed at nonbookish audiences. Historical inevitability had been a prevailing theme in McLuhan's published work and, in its face, frequent appeals for change are sounded. But the notion that there is "absolutely no inevitability" or that "a willingness to contemplate what is happening" might alter the course of historical development puts a voluntarist spin on McLuhan's thought in line with the "can do" tone of his recent addresses to business leaders.

the text in an average book wouldn't do. The medium, after all, was the message.[60]

By inventorying the effects of change in a playful and accessible vein that, though couched in the phototypo-graphical vernacular of the present, is squarely aimed at **you** and your everyday life, the book manages both **to entertain and to initiate a process of cognitive retooling**. To this end, it demands of readers a nonlinear approach to reading, based on the very forms of verbal-visual pattern recognition that McLuhan believed essential to survival and success in the second half of the twentieth century.

anatomies

Three characteristics emerge in the opening sequence that shape the whole of "the first book designed for the TV age":[61]

— a high degree of *self-reference*
— *eclecticism* as a design strategy, and
— an emphasis on *the human body* (as the site where media "imprint" their messages).

The first has already been documented in the case of *The Medium Is the Massage* and will recur in all of Agel's subsequent INVENTORY BOOKS. It takes the form of self-portrayals on the part of the coauthor and coordinator, clippings with direct or oblique ties to the thinker/coauthor's work, and inside jokes. Outstanding among such gestures is the inclusion of an angled page of shorthand from a reporter's notepad on page 116. The handwriting is Agel's and, in addition to containing the names of John Cage and John Lennon (who are about to make cameo appearances on pp. 119, 128, and 137), it performs yet another inconspicuous if complicitous wink. The initials H.M. and H.M.M. and the abbreviation U.M. figure prominently throughout a document that seems to concern deals in which Agel is operating as McLuhan's agent-promoter.[62]

By *eclecticism*, I am pointing in particular to Fiore's promiscuous mixing of sometimes arcane historical materials with clippings from the contemporary press. In no small part this mixing was the result of the fast pace at which Agel and Fiore were forced to work. The text was drafted in little more than a month or two, with another couple of months dedicated to executing the design and layout. Fiore had neither photo lettering nor computer lettering. The budgets for production and artwork were relatively modest: so much so that both coauthor and coordinator were required "to do some arm twisting" to bring the volume to completion.[63]

Yet there was also method in the rush. To craft a book that "predicts the present" by inventorying its effects, a book that recounts "what's happening when what's happening is happening," the new had to meet the now. Informational freshness was of the essence. In his September 1966 "Cocktail Party" column, Agel boasted: "McLuhan's next book, *The Medium Is the Massage*—yes, *the Massage*— co-authored with Quentin Fiore, will be published this autumn by Bantam Books and will include **observations on events as recent as the last week in August**."[64]

Though six months of subsequent publisher's delays ended up compromising this claim to actuality, Fiore's cuts and pastes are firmly situated within the media cycle stretching from the second half of 1965 through the first half of 1966. The printed egg from the January 24, 1966, issue of *Newsweek* is thus in the company of several other near-contemporaneous borrowings: the LOVE dress on page 78 (culled from an April 25, 1966, feature, "*The Story of Pop,*" about McLuhan); the photograph of William F. Buckley's mayoral campaign on page 79 (November 1, 1965); and the voiceprints on page 118 (April 25, 1966). Likewise, the many clippings from the *New York Times* as well as the cartoons reprinted from *Saturday Review* and the *New Yorker* are all from 1965–66. There are other media crisscrossings as well, like the photograph of Niki de Saint-Phalle's *Hon* at Stockholm's Moderna Museet, spread out by Fiore over four pages (pp. 133–36) in *The Medium Is the Massage* but already present on the August 1966 cover of *Books*.

These trappings of "what's happening now" are inter- spliced with borrowings of various sorts. Some are the unmistakable products of Fiore's knowledge of the history of printing: a left-handed scribe at work on page 48 drawn from the frontispiece of Sigismondo Fanti, *Theorica et pratica de modo scribendi fabricandique omnes literarum* (1515); three seventeenth-century gentlemen on page 69, each establishing his own distinctive perspective through a pyramid of strings, an illustration by Abraham Bosse from Gérard Desargues's *Manière universelle pour pratiquer la perspective* (1647). Others alternate the work of well-established photographers and photojournalists (Lewis Hine, Charles Lee Moore, N. R. Farbman, Steve Schapiro) with stock photos (of W. C. Fields, the Kennedy funeral) and stock clip art (arrows, circles, rulers) probably from the then-standard Dover source books.

Within this **motley mix of the high and low, the erudite and the mass cultural, the historical and the contemporary**, a unifying seam is provided by the succession of studio photographs produced for the book by Peter Moore. Numbering fifteen in all, most are the product of a single 1966 photo shoot in a studio with the same two models, one female, one male. Portrayed against a simple white or black backdrop, the models' bodies never appear whole, occurring instead as a sequence of fractured forms: a mechanically multiplied nose, two thumbs holding "the book" open, an eye, a bust, an anamorphically distended face, a pair of fishnet-clad upper legs, two kissing faces, a face with an ear that has rotated forward around the head and into an eye socket. Here, as in the book's many other portrayals of body parts, Fiore provides an overall mapping of how the human sensorium is stretched, stressed, and shaped by the new age. McLuhan's notion of "altered sense ratios," perhaps one of his most elusive (not to mention flawed), is brought down from the ether of historical speculation to the everydayness of **you—your neighborhood—your job** through this constant cataloguing of the human body. From egg to earth, from the single face to multifaceted reality of the Mass Age, *The Medium Is the Massage* diagnoses and anatomizes the contemporary individual.

tailings

Within six months of its publication, first as a paperback original and, two weeks later, as a hardcover, *The Medium Is the Massage*, a project rejected by seventeen publishers and on which even Bantam had placed design restrictions, was already in its eleventh printing and approaching sales of half a million copies. The happening was in full bloom, with both Agel and Fiore swept up in the train of McLuhan's newfound celebrity.

Reviews were plentiful but mixed, most heavily conditioned by the critic's prior attitude toward McLuhan. Some, like Kitman, smelled a con job: "With all the zeal of a convert, **I would like to urge everybody** *not* **to buy this book**, in either the paper medium or the cloth medium."[65] (Kitman's dismissal became the star of Agel's *Decide for Yourself* campaign, always juxtaposed with a rave review.) Others covered a wide spectrum of opinion:

> The book, which is designed by Quentin Fiore and consists of photo and typographical tricks (including mirror type and a recorded voiceprint quiz), McLuhanistic cartoons and quotes from all over (from A. N. Whitehead to Bob Dylan, from Socrates to Sukarno), as well as Mr. McLuhan's abbreviated deadpan, but not wholly unexcitable, text, or litany. If its purpose is to clarify, involve us in and overwhelm us with the effects of the new "Electric Age"—what Mr. McLuhan says we are in without knowing it—it must be said that **it succeeds**. (Eliot Fremont-Smith, *New York Times*)[66]

> The authors of this eye-stopping, mind-wrenching whatzis have created **the ultimate in non-books**. Canada's All-Purpose Prophet Marshall McLuhan, soon to be enchaired at Fordham University, has argued for years that the book is obsolescent. Unfortunately, his major testaments (*The Gutenberg Galaxy*; *Understanding Media*), while full of ideas, were rendered virtually unreadable by soporific

syntax and mastodonian metaphors. [Now] McLuhan gets his message across more appropriately by juxtaposing his text with pictures. The result is a punchy put-on, to be sure, but that only serves to make a point: McLuhan has never taken himself as seriously as his critics have; his cheerful objective is to stir up some fresh thought. (*Time*)[67]

As you read it, as you see it, and almost hear it—you are assaulted by the jangle of McLuhan paragraphs against Fiore graphics. It's like one vast stomach acid commercial—equally unsettling, equally bizarre, equally persuasive [yes, and they do sell a *lot* of Alka Seltzer].... As a book that proves its own point, as an example of itself, *The Medium Is the Massage* must surely constitute some kind of publishing milestone. (Clarence Petersen, *Chicago Tribune*)[68]

In preparing this primer of McLuhanism, the leader has enlisted the ingenious assistance of the designer Quentin Fiore, who does his best through the manipulation of type and image to simulate electronic effects in a print medium and thereby to facilitate our escape from the bonds of the typographical culture. What then is McLuhanism? It is a chaotic combination of bland assertion, astute guesswork, fake analogy, dazzling insight, hopeless nonsense, shockmanship, showmanship, wisecracks, and oracular mystification, all mingling cockily and indiscriminately in an endless and random monologue. It also, in my judgment, contains a deeply serious argument. (Arthur Schlesinger Jr., *Book Week*)[69]

The Medium Is the Massage is a heroic effort to de-book the core ideas of *Understanding Media*. Though it remains an archaic book, it is at least 50% non-verbal. It bears the subtitle *An Inventory of Effects*, and his collaborator is Quentin Fiore, a well-known graphics designer, who tries to make visual the concepts that are verbal in the highly compressed…text. The book is not edited but "co-ordinated" by Jerome Agel. And it works. The—you should excuse the expression—book is striking and confounding, as intended. (Edmund Fuller, *Wall Street Journal*)[70]

The counterpoint between word and image makes *The Medium Is the Massage* a more engaging work than *Understanding Media*. In spite of the brilliant *aperçus* which illuminated almost every chapter of the earlier book, it was written in incredibly graceless prose for a literary scholar who believes that eloquence is the mark of a truly educated man. The need for economy dictated by the alternation of picture and text in the present work probably imposed a healthy discipline on the author's naturally discursive imagination. (Neil Compton, *The Nation*)[71]

Reading [McLuhan] is rather like undergoing an hallucination…. [He] is a monomaniac who happens to be hooked on something extremely important. We ought to be grateful. But the colossal evasiveness, the slipshod reasoning and weak-kneed glibness accompanying the mania make him dangerous going. He has rapidly acquired the reputation of being a prophet, or a charlatan, or both. In fact, he is neither. Capable of the most brilliant and stimulating insight into relationships other historians and social theorists have ignored, he systematically fails to develop this insight critically. Consequently, his view of the connection between media and society is an unbelievable shambles: his dream-logic turns necessary conditions into sufficient conditions, half-truths into sure things, the possible into a fait accompli. (Tom Nairn, *New Statesman*)[72]

The slightly vulgar-successful graphics-design style of Quentin Fiore matches up beautifully with the new Manhattanized McLuhan model. Fiore's work has a subtle element of coarseness which may perhaps be perceived

by comparing his arrows on pp. 40–41 with the very similar design which graces the covers of UNESCO's Mass
Communications publications, or by studying closely the
alphabet on the telephone dial in comparison with that
which Eric Gill (I believe) designed for London Transport's
public signs. It makes of *The Medium Is the Massage*
that strident, snappy, show-bizzy image which is McLuhan
today. McLuhan is becoming the medium: it will be interesting to see what his future creative collaborators make out of
him. (Anthony W. Hodgkinson, *A V Communication Review*)[73]

Though variably sympathetic to McLuhan's intellectual style, critical opinion was, on the whole, favorably
disposed toward Agel and Fiore's phototypographical
translation of the Terrific Torontian's thought. Not always
so, however, within the book arts community. At one well-
attended talk at the Boston Society of Printers, coauthor
Fiore found himself shouted down by hecklers: "They
thought it [*The Medium Is the Massage*] flippant; they
thought it superficial: everything that a book should not
be." Support was forthcoming from university quarters
such as departments of comparative literature, says Fiore,
but "**the design people came only later**."[74]

There were, of course, notable exceptions. Phyllis
Johnson, the former editor of *Women's Wear Daily* and
Advertising Age, was one of them and commissioned a
remix of the book for her avant-garde design review *Aspen*.
The issue assumed the form of a poster-sized press
proof, accompanied by documents on the new tribalism
(the Avalon Ballroom "Tribal Stomp" in San Francisco),
tactility (a nature "Braille Trail"), electronic culture (a
recording of electronic music), antienvironmentalism
(the outlaw biker), information (John Cage's diaries), and
an advertising packet, all designed by Fiore, as per the
standard *Aspen* formula, to fit tidily into a box.[75]

The issue was advertised in the *New York Times* as "Marshall McLuhan was here. He left a message for you." A message for—

you
your neighborhood,
your job,
your government,
your planet.

**and
now
for
something
something
COMPLETELY
different...**

D5575 * $1.65 * A BANTAM BOOK

Marshall McLuhan
Quentin Fiore

authors of the electrifying bestseller
THE MEDIUM IS THE MASSAGE

war and
peace
in the
global village

Co-ordinated by
Jerome Agel

Our Global Village:

It's possible, even today, to encounter highly educated people who are quite unaware that only phonetically literate man lives in a "rational" or "pictorial" space. The discovery or invention of such space that is uniform, continuous, and connected was an environmental effect of the phonetic alphabet in the sensory life of ancient Greece. This form of rational or pictorial space is an environment that results from no other form of writing, Hebraic, Arabic, or Chinese.

Now that we live in an electric environment of information coded not just in visual but in other sensory modes, it's natural that we now have new perceptions that destroy the monopoly and priority of visual space, making this older space look as bizarre as a medieval coat of arms over the door of a chemistry lab.

New environments inflict considerable pain on the perceiver. Biologists and physicists are much more aware of the radical revolution effected in our senses by new technological environments than are the literati, for whom the new environments are more threatening than for those in other disciplines.

When print was new in the sixteenth century, Hieronymus Bosch painted the new confusion of spaces resulting from the Gutenberg technology invasion of the old tactile world of medieval iconography. His "horror" pictures are a faithful artistic report of the pain and misery that result from a new technology. Even at the popular level, the confusion and pain created by radio in the twenties was lavishly expressed in the blues. Today, with television, a much more powerful medium, pain has

... experiencing a jolting series of prearranged disappointments, down the long lane of ... generations, ... FW 107.

The solid man saved by his sillied woman. Cracka-jolking away like a hearse on fire. FW 94.

All human progress is a result of standing on the shoulders of our predecessors.

Alexander was a dropout from Aristotle's university

To speed his armies, Napoleon made all his countries drive on the right-hand side of the road

Napoleon had very much the same tribal background as Alexander, but it was one tinged by the European eighteenth century. For example, Napoleon was enthusiastic about Rousseau, who taught a primitive tribalism as a basis for human unity and happiness. Like many a semiliterate, Napoleon was prolific in inventions. His semaphore telegraph carried messages from Rome to Paris in four hours, giving him a huge advantage over his enemies. Perhaps most extraordinary of all was his insistence in the interest of speed that everybody keep to the right-hand side of the road in order to expedite and simplify traffic problems. Where his armies went, right-hand driving has remained, even in Russia. He never got to Sweden, and the Swedes didn't switch to the right-hand side until 1967. He never got to England, and they still drive on the left-hand side. But even in Napoleon's day, the English had probably developed too big a stake in their own way of driving to make any transition possible.

Hiroshima watch
—Moment of Truth

"...space we can recover, time never;...

I may lose a battle, but I shall never lose a minute..."

"The Campaigns of Napoleon," by David G. Chandler. Copyright © David G. Chandler 1964. The Macmillan Company, Weidenfeld & Nicolson, Ltd.

This insistence on rapid movement as a basic principle of war highlights another of Napoleon's master concepts—the vital significance of time and its accurate calculation in relation to space. "The loss of time is irreparable in war," he once asserted. Considerations of time and distance were the basic calculations underlying all his great strategic moves. "Strategy is the art of making use of time and space. I am less chary of the latter than of the former; space we can recover, time never"; "I may lose a battle, but I shall never lose a minute"; "Time is the great element between weight and force." *The Correspondence* is full of references to this element of warfare as understood by Napoleon. Hours, even days, could be saved or gained by a careful selection of the best routes to the chosen objective. Indeed, Napoleon did not usually demand an unreasonable degree of effort from his marching columns—except, as we have seen, at

(feedback loop)

With the first book for the television age riding high atop the paperback charts, Agel moved forward with the once skeptical publishing industry eagerly in tow. Two follow-up INVENTORY BOOKS were in the pipeline by the summer of 1967: a project built on the same McLuhan/Agel/Fiore tripod and a collaboration with R. Buckminster Fuller.

The first of these projects had been in development since the end of the prior year when, as noted earlier, a contract "almost identical to the *Massage* contract" had been drawn up for a work titled *The Effects of Automation*. "Quentin and I have started to outline the work," wrote Agel on November 23, 1966. "Whom and what companies would you like us to contract for reports and information on automation effects?"[76] The path from this initial planning exercise to the formal announcement in the December 1967 issue of *Books* of "a new book by Marshall McLuhan and Quentin Fiore [titled] *Keep in Touch: War and Peace in the Global Village*" due out "next year" is complex, if only because a third McLuhan/Agel/Fiore book on the subject of education seems to have partly merged with *Keep in Touch*.[77] The latter resurfaces three months later in an article titled "McLuhan Recovers from Major Operation, Writes New Book," with the book's title stripped of allusions to tactility and a delayed release date of June 1.

In point of fact, *War and Peace in the Global Village: An Inventory of some of the current spastic situations that could be eliminated by more feedforward*, as the book came to be called, wouldn't appear in print until September 1968. The circumstances that determined the delay were multiple. McLuhan had two other writing projects under-way at the time: *Through the Vanishing Point* was nearing completion; *From Cliché to Archetype* was in prepara-tion. Agel was busily at work as McLuhan's agent, coor-dinating media appearances and speaking engagements, while writing for and running *Books*. Fiore had moved out of New York City to Princeton, New Jersey. Then, in November 1967, in the midst of his tenure as the Albert Schweitzer Professor in the Humanities at Fordham University, a mere subway ride away from Agel Publishing, a twenty-hour operation was required to remove a tumor from McLuhan's brain.

The McLuhan family's proximity decisively altered the book's character. Whereas in the case of *The Medium Is the Massage*, Agel and Fiore worked at a distance, whit-tling down McLuhan's thought to a terse, visually driven argument, seeking his approval only after finalizing each phase of their labors, in the case of *War and Peace in the Global Village* the collaboration was closer, with face-to-face meetings the norm. Eric McLuhan remembers the project's unfolding as follows:

> Jerry proposed the book and he and Dad worked up a list of topics. That list became the heads in the book. Jerry started the list; Dad added to it and revised it and so on. Dad then took the list and wrote a small essay under each heading. I was present at several meetings between the three of them. Those meetings always went smoothly and amiably. Quentin was quite professional about his work, not the emotional *artiste*; so he was easy to work with. Jerry, too, was full of suggestions. Consequently, meetings tended

to become lively idea sessions, until Jerry broke in with an item of business.[78]

Rather than a second "comprehensive contraction," *War and Peace in the Global Village* quickly evolved into a new book *by* McLuhan assisted by collaborators. As such, unlike *The Medium Is the Massage* ("I didn't write anything for that book"), McLuhan never hesitated to claim *War and Peace* as his own. On December 15, 1967, he wrote to family friends Philip and Molly Deane:

> Have a new book, just about ready, called *War and Peace in the Global Village*. The sub-plot is the effect of the computer. The main plot is simply that every new technology creates a new environment that alters the perceptual life of the entire population. Since violence is the inevitable means of quest for identity when the old image, private or corporate, is smudged by the new technology, war is automatic as a means of recovering identity.[79]

The same sense of ownership spills over into a letter written two weeks later to then vice president Hubert Humphrey, that recapitulates the book's arguments with respect to the first TV war (Vietnam): "My theme is War and Peace in the Global Village."[80]

Thanks to the active authorial role assumed by McLuhan, the resulting book is more literary/scholarly than magazinelike. Text predominates over visuals, occupying four times more graphic real estate than it did in *The Medium Is the Massage*. Blank spaces are reduced to a minimum. The same 4⅜" × 7" format is maintained, but the page count balloons from 160 to 192 pages. A paratextual apparatus made up of footnotes, epigrams, and quotations (in a book whose main text is itself a mosaic of quotations) invades the margins. Tapping into the wisdom of Bertrand Russell, William Butler Yeats, B. F. Skinner,

George Bernard Shaw, and the comedian Pat Paulsen, the apparatus highlights ninety-three extracts from James Joyce's *Finnegans Wake*. The aim was **to let "Joyce comment in person on the text from the sidelines,"** as Eric McLuhan describes it, and pages 46–48 feature Eric's own typographical tabulation of the ten thunders of the *Wake*: the result of years of joint reading and research on the part of father and son.[81] The same thunders also rumble across the chapter title pages where the black-and-white photograph of a lightning strike (always placed on the page's verso) appears with the title set in white on the lower right. Joyce was McLuhan's oracle, collaborator, and laboratory. Eric notes that "he did not merely use Joyce to confirm an insight, but also used Joyce as the stimulus for fresh awareness of the present moment."[82] It is, accordingly, Joyce who structures McLuhan's *Inventory of some of the current spastic situations that could be eliminated by more feedforward.*

The shift toward a more textcentric model of the INVENTORY BOOK implied a recalibration of Fiore's coauthorship. *War and Peace in the Global Village* was "a continuance of the relationship," Fiore would later declare; "it was a milder kind of book…[in which] I didn't play that great a role"; or, rather, Fiore found himself recast in the role of *researcher* as much as designer.[83] He wrote McLuhan on August 14, 1967:

> Practically all of my time for the past few months has been devoted to "burrowing"—digging out **many beautiful and kooky "facts"** for our use. A huge pile of material has been reduced down to a manageable size—it's all **fresh material.** [Firestone Library, newspapers and conversations with friends who are doing pioneer work in computer technology, psychiatry, and neurology, etc.] A lot of stuff has been gathered on computer technology and logic, man-machine interface, artificial intelligence, "problem-solving," [change, habit,

anxiety-fear, etc.], facial expressions, olfaction as communication, thought control, the synaptic process, work/leisure,
wife-swapping, etc., etc., etc., etc., etc., etc., etc.—all this
plus an up-to-date, science non-fiction collection of "hard-
ware" [edible, miniaturized TV sets for diagnosis].

I've been calling Jerry everyday and have been meet-
ing with him in NYC once a week. We are both very excited
and we feel assured that we have an enormously exciting
book—and very different from "Massage."[84]

In the fall, Fiore's materials were merged with eight
pages of typed notes composed of aphorisms, images,
and sources for quotations redacted on the basis of a series
of meetings between McLuhan, Agel, and Fiore. These
were organized into three thematic nuclei, initially titled
"The Global Village," "Not with a Bang but a Whimper," and
"Fearful Symmetry," to which was added a conclusion.

Though the shape and composition of the nuclei
would mutate during the drafting process—a process during which McLuhan and Agel were continually inserting
new materials culled from the press into the typescript—
they would eventually come to form the backbone of a
finalized book whose argument hinges on the relationship between technological change (including automation) and education. Its structure may be schematized
as follows—

4–5	Prefatory note on marginalia from *Finnegans Wake*	
8–95	Our Global Village	nucleus 1
96–147	War as Education	nucleus 2
148–55	Education as War	nucleus 3
156–73	The Bore War	nucleus 3
174–87	A Message to the Fish	conclusion
188–90	Appendix: A Message to the Fish Fresh Out of Water	

nucleus 1 details changes in the environment, the role of art in adaptation, and **the transformative power of technologies from the stirrup to the mainframe computer** (which promises to complete the transformation of the world into humanity's virtual limb). Spastic movements, both figurative and literal, are the result of the defective feedback loops that arise when a powerful new prosthetic extension of humanity, such as the computer, is forced to adapt *backward* (i.e., reactively) to a diversity of older, maladapted technologies. These defective loops could eventually be remedied in a more feed*forward* future, or so the text implies.

nucleus 2 reveals McLuhan at his most Paul Virilio–like as he describes **war as a gesture of self-defense in the face of a pervasive sense of threat and fear of injury.** After this follow accounts of Napoleon's transformation of military tactics and education, of the role of war as engine of economic growth and agent of compulsory modernization,

and of how communications technologies determine the character of individual wars (railways ›› WWI; radio ›› WWII; television ›› WWIII/Vietnam). The nucleus closes with a lengthy rumination on Hermann Hesse's *Siddhartha* and the disenchantment of contemporary youth, suggesting that Hesse's tale provides not an alternative but an ascetic double of the war establishment's bellicose striving for a secure sense of self.

nucleus 3 was the most heterogeneous from the outset and ends up split into two sections. (A third section header, "The Playing Fields of Eton," was foreseen at p. 168 but eliminated before printing.) Here the narrative shifts gears in jarring fashion. The central theme is **education as the older generation's war against the young**: as a last-ditch battle to defend the status quo in the face of overwhelming change that provokes, in turn, a wholesale revolt on the part of youth. "The Bore War" translates the conflict into the language of fashion: traditional fashion, much like armor, is a form of weaponry that separates and protects; the fashions of today join together, uncover, and bring skin into closer contact with skin. Like the games and sports that people play in contemporary society, they expose and explore the contours of a new tribal society in which tactile values are privileged over visual/analytic skills.

"A Message to the Fish" appears to have been written last and doesn't figure in McLuhan's early notes. Graphically differentiated from the theme of Joycean thunder by a title page that shows not lightning but a catfish swimming through a tangle of plant life, it explores the ultimate promise of the artificial environment within which humanity swims: the total history that, thanks to electronics, "is now potentially present in a kind of simultaneous transparency.... We have been rapt in 'the artifice of eternity' by the placing of our own nervous system throughout the globe" (p. 177). Whereas for tens of centuries humankind had evolved within an environment that was broken up into ever-smaller pieces, the electric revolution "inevitably drives us back into a world of mythic vision in which we put Humpty Dumpty back together again" (p. 185). Quoting from William Blake's *Apocalypse*, the conclusion gestures darkly toward the advent of an irenic future: perhaps too darkly, given that a brief appendix was slotted in as an afterthought. Here the promise is brought into sharper focus: thanks to the global unity achieved through the triumph of computing as humanity's all-encompassing environment, a time may be approaching when the universe merges into a single organism and humanity will attain a "macrocosmic connubial bliss derided by the evolutionist" (p. 190).

· · ·

War and Peace in the Global Village thus leads the reader from Paradise Lost to Paradise Regained, proposing a sweeping, if jaggedly kaleidoscopic, account of the roots of and remedies to human violence. The path is studded with ideational leaps, memorable one-liners, and striking visuals cast in the same eclectic pop-surrealist vein as *The Medium Is the Massage*. But the going is sometimes less than smooth. There are traces of last-minute improvisation: one appendix to the book was nixed, another added; the passages on Frantz Fanon's *Studies in a Dying Colonialism* (pp. 99–102, 157–59) were patched in late, perhaps in response to Grove Press's recent publication of *Black Skin, White Masks*; a program of newspaper headlines had to be dropped; the overall visual and verbal rhythms of the book can seem choppy.

Working with only nine "iconic" double spreads and twenty-two full-page visuals (including the chapter title pages), Fiore opts for a more conventional iconographic strategy instead of the modes of visual argumentation favored in *The Medium Is the Massage*. He builds the book around not an abecedarium of fragments of the human body but instead the mapping of intersections between humanity and the animal world in support of the text's evolutionary/postevolutionary theme.[85] Images of individuals engaged in individual and collective actions are thus intermingled with a long succession of animal pictures: a shrieking monkey (pp. 14–15), a flea (p. 17), a camel (p. 24), horses (pp. 30, 32–33, 38, 109), a crab (p. 57), a gorilla (p. 87), a spider (p. 130), a dove (p. 137), a fish (p. 174), a lion (p. 187), and a turtle (p. 192). These appear in the company of the same dynamic mix of stock photos, advertisements, and cartoons, though stripped of the self-reflexivity of the inaugural INVENTORY BOOK (with respect to *Books*, to its creators, and to the act of reading). The *tesserae* pulsate with local life, the interaction between text and image remains lively, but do they trend together toward that "integral mosaic vision" (p. 186) whose coming the book prophecies to the sound of irenic trumpets?

Critical opinion was split. Tom Wolfe recognized *War and Peace in the Global Village* as a major stepping stone toward "a Master Theory...on the scale of a Darwin or a Nietzsche" and praised McLuhan's "marvelous Nietzsche-like gift for aphorisms," but sounded a note of caution about the wobbly scientific foundations of McLuhan's claims for sensory ratios.[86] From the pages of the *Wall Street Journal*, Edmund Fuller lauded it as "a book that shakes up the mind," describing McLuhan as "head sooth-sayer of the electronic age, and the sooth that he says is disquieting and undoubtedly important, even though it is at times hard to understand, either because it is cryptic or because he writes a heavy-weather prose."[87] Paul D. Zimmerman gathered together the dissenting opinions on the pages of *Newsweek*:

> McLuhan's latest non-book...is a perfect target for his prosecutors. Its sins are those of his first pictorial non-book *The Medium Is the Massage*, also done with graphic designer Quentin Fiore. He again produces what British critic Anthony Quinton calls a "thin diet of prose...eked out with a great deal of typographic space-wastage and photographic interruptions, in an attempt to produce something nearer to the specifications of his theory." He presents what Dwight Macdonald damns as "impure nonsense, adulterated by sense." And he decorates the margins of his text with snatches from *Finnegans Wake* that bear no apparent relation to anything at all.[88]

Zimmerman was joined by Fremont-Smith, whose "The Tedium Is the Message" also observed that "whatever else it is, McLuhanism has become its own little industry—a trifle passé, perhaps, a trifle tedious, but clearly thriving still. Yet it need no longer be intimidating. Indeed, he may wake up one morning to find it has all blown away, like so much swamp gas."[89] From academic quarters the book was greeted by the firing of repeated rounds of heavy artillery in the direction of Toronto.

In short, plenty of fodder for Agel, who now replayed the earlier *Decide for Yourself* campaign in various guises. The summer 1968 issue of *Books*, for instance, experimented with a swarm-based promotional model, scattering mini-"insights" across the entire issue, each consisting in a single McLuhan aperçu, all referenced back to a root advertisement. These were followed by ads, after the book's publication, headlined by the question "What if he is wrong?": a reversal of the title of Wolfe's celebrated 1965 profile "What if he is right?" The "Bore War" section of the book was prepublished in the *Saturday Evening Post*. [90] The book sold reasonably well, though nowhere near the levels of *The Medium Is the Massage*: was this the first sign of a rising tide of McLuhan fatigue?

Insight

"Violence in its many forms, as an involuntary quest for identity, has in our time come to reveal the meaning of war in entirely new guise."

(See Page Eleven)

Insight

"The Depression of 1930 is nothing compared to the slump that is just beginning with the aid of television."

(See Page Eleven)

Perhaps. Yet, for the moment, the "little industry" continued to boom: so much so that Agel was finding it difficult to sustain the one-man show that was *Books*. By the end of the year the monthly ceased publication (though he sought to relaunch it in 1970 as a weekly newspaper titled *Keep in Touch*).[91] "The Cocktail Party" found a temporary home on the pages of Paul Krassner's *Realist*, where it appeared in December 1968 and April 1969, only to resurface as an occasional contribution to the *Washington Post*'s "Book Buzz." Agel's focus shifted to growing the INVENTORY BOOKS franchise. He cooked up new McLuhan projects almost monthly, as well as reaching out to the likes of Elias Canetti, from whose recently translated *Crowds and Power* he developed a page of excerpts plus illustrations "from the planned *massage* version," which was promptly published much as he had done years earlier with McLuhan.[92] The future McLuhan projects came to naught. No Canetti/Agel/Fiore book ever materialized. But…**good morning!**…another dormant comprehensive contraction just woke up.

Environment and man's future—
by the visionary genius of our time—

R. Buckminster Fuller

I Seem To Be A Verb

R. Buckminster Fuller with Jerome Agel and Quentin Fiore

"The most important fact about Spaceship Earth:
An instruction book didn't come with it."

The most important fact about Spaceship Earth: An instruction book didn't come with it.

I am convinced that creativity is *a priori* to the integrity of universe and that life is regenerative and conformity meaningless.

Man can approximate the magnificent efficiencies and economies of the macro-micro tensional integrities of nature.

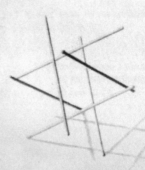

I always say to myself, what is the most important thing we can think about at this extraordinary moment.

The new life needs to be inspired with the realization that the new advantages were gained through great gropes in the dark by unknown, unsung intellectual explorers.

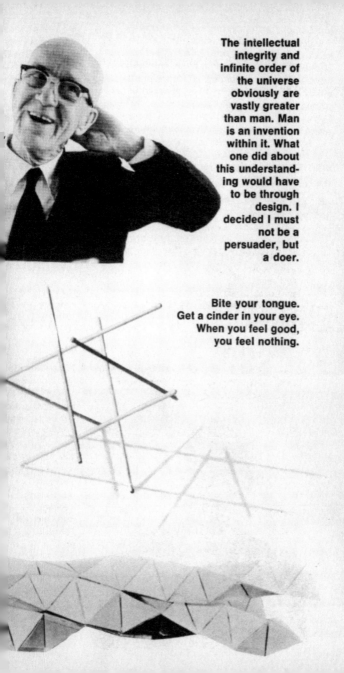

The intellectual integrity and infinite order of the universe obviously are vastly greater than man. Man is an invention within it. What one did about this understanding would have to be through design. I decided I must not be a persuader, but a doer.

Bite your tongue. Get a cinder in your eye. When you feel good, you feel nothing.

Most of our value systems — for example, the concept of gold as essential to economic control — are lethal and obsolete. These inheritances have been retained jealously by communists and capitalists alike, who maintain control by promulgating them as natural and fundamental laws. How many millions have been slaughtered for gold found on their lands?

Square tomato.

A master tool maker in India should be paid the same wage as a master tool maker in Detroit.

"Let them eat cak
—MARIE ANTOINET

"I sometimes feel as though I'm playing center field with people hitting fly balls to me all at once."—*Robert W. Haac 10 months after taking over the presidency of the New Yor Stock Exchange.*

LEMS ARE WORLD PROE

MS. MAN KNOWS SO MU

GRESSIVELY BURDENSO

"Do you have a bag I can put his estate in?"

When people discard th[e] notion that ownership is im[-]portant, they will not b[e] burdened with possession[s]. The less we own, the great[er] our mobility. Possession [of] most things will seem a[s] illogical as owning a tel[e]phone.

"Any kind of recreation or hobby helps, because it keeps your mind busy. Hard work of any kind diminishes sex interest, and hard physical work can make you forget about it entirely. You will notice this at time when your training is most intensive."
—*Army Life, U.S. Government Printing Office, 1944.*

• •

It will be cheaper to capture and re-use the chemicals being spewed from industrial smoke stacks than it will be to redress the abuses of air pollution.

Man wears blinders. He rarely sees beyond his feed bag.

• •

"One could only conclude that the management of your intelligence assets is in a state of complete disarray."—*Representative James L. Whitten to Defense Intelligence Agency officials who had reported that spies were collecting information so fast that the chiefs did not have time to read it.*

CH DOES SO LITTLE.
ION IS BECOMING PRO

braham Lincoln's concept of "Right Triumphing Over Might" as realized when Einstein as metaphysical intellect wrote the ual of physical universe, $E = MC^2$, and thus comprehended it.

EPHEMERALIZATION

The process of doing more with less.

Ephemeralization: One Telstar—weighing only 500 pounds—out-performing 75,000 tons of transocean copper cable.

Ephemeralization has flourished in different systems, for it is independent of political ideology.

Automation, initiated by the mass production of electronics, has generated an awareness of the significance of ephemeralization.

"History is **bunk**." —HENRY FORD.

"We've looked so long at rigid lines of print—people are more willing now to accept the illogical." —MERCE CUNNINGHAM.

EATEST FACT OF CENT
EEN REALIZED. POSSE

There are two kinds of inventions—those that increase mobilit... (little red wagons, blimps, canoes) and those that inhibit mobilit... (straightjackets, handcuffs, stone walls). It's far easier to inven... means of mobility—up to 186,000 miles per second—than it i... to invent limits on mobility.

ditto

The cover of the same December 1967 issue of *Books* that trumpeted the upcoming publication of *War and Peace in the Global Village* included a second announcement:

> Buckminster Fuller is a 72-year-old engineer, inventor, mathematician, architect, cartographer, philosopher, poet, cosmogonist, comprehensive designer, and choreographer—doing the twist, he has sailed right off a yacht into the Aegean Sea—whose ideas were once considered wildly visionary. His views presented here are from a variety of sources made available by Mr. Fuller to Bantam Books for a "Massage"-type original paperback for publication next year.

Negotiated at the start of 1966 but reactivated thanks to Bantam's support, the book in question would actually appear two and one-half years later under the title *I Seem to Be a Verb*.[93] Its title page attests to a realignment: it is signed R. Buckminster Fuller *with* Jerome Agel and Quentin Fiore. No "producer" or "coordinator" is listed. There were also two design assistants on the project: Cathryn S. Aison and Peter Renich; the first developed the majority of the mechanicals, with the latter finalizing them.[94]

The expanded team suggests an increased level of support from Bantam and grander design ambitions. The shift in credits suggests Agel's decreasing willingness to cast himself as a behind-the-scenes player and Fiore's struggle to juggle the many opportunities coming his way with Agel's mile-a-minute projects, especially now that he was working out of his home studio in Princeton. After this last of their collaborations, Agel would produce another half-dozen INVENTORY BOOKS on his own. Fiore gradually turned to designing leather-bound editions of literary classics. Their friendship remained as strong as ever, even if they were now neither next-door neighbors nor collaborators.

Third in the Agel/Fiore trilogy, *I Seem to Be a Verb* is the most complex in its verbal/visual/typographic layerings. If *The Medium Is the Massage* is a guide to the television era for the perplexed and *War and Peace in the Global Village* is the Terrific Torontian's Book of Electric Revelations, *I Seem to Be a Verb* is a **FAST-PACED CRAZY QUILT** of late-1960s life, with Fuller serving as pretext and glue. The book abandons any lingering pretense of linear argumentation in the name of an unabashedly cinematic, jump-cut, montage-based approach. As Aison put it in a recent telephone interview, "The motivation was to create a kind of storyboard: a book that could compete with film without being a film, made up of dissolves and quick cuts."[95] The ostensible theme is pure Bucky—"for the first time, man has the chance to be a complete success in his environment"—and the building blocks are Fullerisms in variably sized chunks: from aphorisms ("everyone is born an inventor") to extended passages like the definition of man from *Nine Chains to the Moon* that appears full page on 66b.[96]

The book's substance, however, is continuous with the agenda of the prior volumes. *I Seem to Be a Verb* "is based on Fuller's present concepts, ideas, philosophies, inventions," Agel declares in an interview with Chuck Pulin.

"[L]ike *The Medium Is the Massage*…this new book is designed to put into popular form, or into more understandable form, some of the great ideas of our times. It lays out what the future could be like if we recognize the truth of situations."[97] Shaping the future by "recognizing the truth of situations" sounds just like the agenda of *The Medium Is the Massage*: shunning inevitability through a "willingness to contemplate what is happening."

And it is. No more than a quarter of the overall content in *I Seem to Be a Verb* derives from Fuller. The rest is pure Agel and Fiore: a patchwork of three hundred verbal quotations interwoven with another several hundred visual quotations; an encyclopedia of typefaces extending from courier to **futura** to various *cursives* and *italics* to handwritten scribbles in point sizes ranging from ₄ to

48;

dividing bars, decorative borders, and dingbats of every description arrayed along variable axes; a scattering of self-referential elements (a picture of Agel's son with a cubical papier-mâché mask on his head is on p. 177a; a postcard from Agel's daughter on p. 108b; an Aison photo on p. 182b); multiple carryovers of messages and materials from the prior McLuhan books ("Speak that I may see you" [p. 61a], Whitehead, Carroll, Joyce), as well as from the pages of Agel's *Books* (Canetti, Kubrick, the photographs on pp. 148–49 and 176a, the cartoons on pp. 102b–101b).

A quick glance at the following source index (limited to the text alone) reveals the dizzying diversity of the materials assembled—

Exactly how and by whom these materials were developed remains uncertain, though the range and quantity point mostly in the direction of Agel, whose restless mental habits and love of quotation arrays are well documented on the pages of *Books*. The book's core design concepts, as well as some of the layouts, are surely the work of Fiore (and there seem to be many borrowings from Fiore's research for *War and Peace in the Global Village*).

Whatever the exact division of duties, this much appears certain: in early October 1969, Agel presented Aison with Fiore's design brief for the book and with a large box containing the visual and textual repertory out of which the book was to be assembled. The schedule was tight: "It took me three months to write the book and prepare a preliminary design; it took six to prepare the 192 mechanicals."[98] There was time for few if any corrections. Fiore was mostly out of the loop during this final stage of the book's development. The sole imperative was *everything ASAP*: out with the book!

To emphasize the scattershot character of the collage and the accelerated production schedule is not to imply a lack of structure, for *I Seem to Be a Verb* possesses a distinctive architecture. It opens with a twelve-page sequence of Fuller quotes and familiar icons interspersed with quotes: Bucky on Bear Island, Maine (1967); some standard tensegrity models; a Marine helicopter lifting a "flying house" (1959). These are intercut with a sequence of stills of Fuller speaking, with the final shot on page 9 picked up again as a half-page image on page 11, where it sits atop the well-known single-sentence two-hundred-word self-description ("What I Am Trying To Do") composed as a *Who's Who* entry.[99] The facing page reproduces a full-page microscopic image of the structure of a single-cell marine creature that echoes the geodesic structures of the prior and successive pages (like the two-page spread, printed in green, on pages 144–45, of "tensegrity geodesic triangulation seen in greatly magnified outer tissue structure of the human testes"). The introduction concludes with the enigmatic juxtaposition of René Magritte's painting *The Lovers* (1928) paired off against a closing set of jumbo quotation marks that frame the sequence as a whole as if it were an extended verbal-visual quotation. (Which is what it is.)

SOCIETY NEITHER HEARS NOR SEES THE GREAT CHANGES GOING ON. EITHER MAN IS OBSOLETE OR WAR IS
POLITICIANS ARE ALWAYS REALISTICALLY MANEUVERING FOR THE NEXT ELECTION. THEY ARE OBSOLE
THRESHOLD INTO HUMAN CONSCIOUSNESS AND ULTIMATE POPULAR SUPPORT. TODAY'S STUDENTS, REARED
THEIRS WILL BE THE MOST POWERFUL CONSTRUCTIVE REVOLUTION IN HISTORY. EARTH IS A VERY SMALL SPACE
BEING ON EARTH. WEAPONRY HAS ALWAYS BEEN ACCORDED PRIORITY OVER LIVINGRY. ONLY TWO ALTERNATIVE
GREATEST FACT OF CENTURY: WE CAN MAKE LIFE ON EARTH GENERAL SUCCESS FOR ALL PEOPLE. WORLD'S P
KILOWATTS MANHOURS OF WORLD'S COMPREHENSIVE RESOURCES, RENDERING THOSE RESOURCES CAPABLE (
THAN ANY HUMAN MINORITY SINGLE INDIVIDUAL HAS KNOWN OR DREAMED OF. WAR OVER POPULATION HUNGE
MALTHUS IS WRONG. THERE IS ENOUGH TO GO AROUND. BASIC YOU-OR-ME-NOT-ENOUGH-FOR-BOTH-ERGO-SOME(
COMBINATION OF PHYSICAL ENERGY AND HUMAN INTELLECT. EVERY TIME WE USE REAL WEALTH IT INC
TO HAVENESS. (IF YOU CAN PRODUCE IT, YOU CAN AFFORD IT. IF YOU CAN'T PRODUCE IT, YOU CAN'T AFFORD
MIND DISCOVERS GENERALIZED PATTERNS APPARENTLY GOVERNING ALL SPECIAL CASE EXPERIENCES. THINKING I S
REVOLUTION IN HUMAN AFFAIRS HAS BEEN ASCENDANCY OF INTELLECT'S INTUITIVE MASTERY OVER THE PHYSICAL
PROBABILITY URELIABLE. TO EACH OF US ENVIRONMENT IS EVERYTHING THAT ISN'T "ME." NEW, PHYSICALLY (
PROVIDED BY THE UTTERLY IMPERSONAL PROBLEM SOLUTIONS OF MAN'S ANTIBODY, THE COMPUTER. ONLY TO
FACE-SAVINGLY ACQUIESCE. EVOLUTION IS APPARENTLY INTENT THAT MAN FULFILL A MUCH GREATER DESTIN
MODERN NATION, HIGHLY AUTOMATED.) AUTOMATION CAN PRODUCE WEALTH BEYOND ALL OUR NEEDS AND DREAMS.
PRODUCTION AND CONTROL SPECIALIST -- JUST IN TIME. SPECIALIZATIONS ONLY A FANCY FORM OF SLAVERY W
CULTURALLY PREFERRED, ERGO, HIGHLY-SECURE. LIFE-LONG POSITION. NATURE ALWAYS DOES THINGS IN SIMP
NATURE DOESN'T HAVE SEPARATE DEPARTMENTS OF PHYSICS, CHEMISTRY, BIOLOGY, MATHEMATICS, WORLD SOC
WHERE CHANGE IS NORMAL. BECAUSE PRIME EVOLUTIONARY TRANSFORMATIONS ARE INVISIBLE, IT IS AP
LAST 100 YEARS, ARTISTS ARE NOW BEING RECOGNIZED AS EXTRAORDINARILY IMPORTANT TO HUMAN SOCI
THE LABORATORIES. EVERY CHILD IS BORN A GENIUS. NINETY-NINE PERCENT ARE DEGENIUSED BY EARLY
ARE BIGGEST "SCHOOL" OPPORTUNITY. CHILD IS TRIM TAB OF THE FUTURE. LEAST FAVORABLE ENVIR
WITHIN 10 YEARS ANYTHING DESIRABLE THINGS-UPABLE BY SCIENCE FICTION WILL PROBABLY HAVE BEEN RE
A TOTAL WAVE OF TRANSFORMATION INTO AN ENTIRELY NEW RELATIONSHIP WITH THE UNIVERSE. MAN FREED O
MUTUAL EFFORTLESSLY IN ONE ANOTHER'S EAR FROM ANYWHERE AROUND THE WORLD. (BE SURE TO ENTERTAIN A
COMMERCIAL SEA. FALSE PREMISE INSTITUTIONS WILL VANISH WITH STARTLING RAPIDITY. MAN, AS DE
EXPERIMENT IS ALWAYS VALUABLE. YOU CAN'T LEARN LESS. YOU CAN ALWAYS GET NEARER TO THE T
IS AHEAD FOR ALL OF US. (MAN WAS DESIGNED WITH LEGS -- NOT ROOTS.) MAN CAN DO ANYTHING HE

At this juncture **the book splits in two, with the upper left-to-right portion printed in black and the lower right-to-left portion printed in green**. The dividing line is established through a double horizontal band that runs the full length of the book, left to right and right to left, like a kind of tickertape composed of Fullerisms. Nearly nine hundred words in length, it reads like an oracle:

```
TIMATE TOOL OF POLITICS. POLITICAL LEADERS LOOK OUT ONLY FOR THEIR OWN SIDE.
AL PROBLEM-SOLVERS. HALF-CENTURY OF SUBCONSCIOUSLY DEVELOPING WORLD REVOLUTION IS CROSSING
"THE THIRD PARENT," THINK WORLD. THEY THINK DEMAND JUSTICE FOR ALL HUMANITY, WITH NO EXCEPTIONS.
ASTRONAUTS. EACH HUMAN IS A WHOLE UNIVERSE. WE HAVE 28,000 POUNDS OF EXPLOSIVES FOR EACH HUMAN
LIVION. ALL THE FUNDAMENTAL PROBLEMS ARE WORLD PROBLEMS. MAN KNOWS SO MUCH DOES SO LITTLE.
EN: HOW TO TRIPLE SWIFTLY SAFELY SATISFYINGLY OVERALL PERFORMANCE REALIZATIONS PER POUNDS
HUNDRED PER CENT OF HUMANITY'S INCREASING POPULATION AT EVER HIGHER STANDARDS OF LIVING
EASE TO EXIST IF "HAVE"S DEVOTED LARGER SHARE OF THEIR INDUSTRIAL BUDGET TO WORLD LIVINGRY.
OF CLASS WARFARING ARE EXTINCT. REAL WEALTH -- INDESTRUCTIBLE, WITHOUT PRACTICAL LIMIT -- IS
MUST INCREASE WEALTH TO ELIMINATE POVERTY DESIGN SCIENCE, INVENTION REVOLUTION COULD ELEVATE POVERTY
CE SHOULD BE RECOGNIZED AS A GLOBAL RESOURCE. BRAIN STORES RETRIEVES SPECIAL CASE EXPERIENCES.
DISCIPLINED SEPARATION OF RELEVANT FEEDBACK FROM IRRELEVANT FEEDBACK. GREATEST SINGLE
ANT CRITICAL EVENTS REALIZING THAT REVOLUTION JUST HAPPENS. ONLY THE IMPOSSIBLE HAPPENS.
PHYSICAL INITIATIVE OF UNBIASED INTEGRITY COULD UNIFY WORLD. IT COULD AND PROBABLY WILL BE
PERHUMAN RANGE OF CALCULATIVE CAPABILITIES CAN AND MAY A
```

The collaged-in elements above and below the line are sometimes keyed to the tickertape or to the other Fuller quotes integrated into the upper or lower portions of the page. More often than not the connections are atmospheric or oblique (if not entirely absent). Ten two-page spreads and twelve full individual pages interrupt the bidirectionality at semiregular intervals, amplifying either the black upper or the green lower zone. As always, the opening and closing are meaningful. The first split page is topped by a quote from Janis Ian: "When I walk onstage, man, all I can give them is me" (p. 13a); the inverted image below, the book's last, is of Fuller's feverish schedule of public lectures (p. 13b). This framing suggests that *I Seem to Be a Verb* is somehow to be read as the record of an existence lived on stage: the lifelong lab experiment carried out by a subject known as Guinea Pig B(ucky).

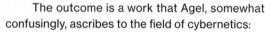

The outcome is a work that Agel, somewhat confusingly, ascribes to the field of cybernetics:

> From pages 13 to 192, the pages are divided in half. You can read one half of each page from 13 to 192 and you can then turn the book around and come back to page 13; or you can start at 192, jump to 13 and come back to 192. Do you follow me? There is a reason for the style. The book discusses how computers could be used to improve our lives. Computers provide immediate feedback of information. **The feedback concept in printed form is used in *I Seem to Be a Verb* to indicate that when you come back on information that you've read five minutes earlier your view of that same information is altered by what you've learned in those last five minutes.**[100]

Though it is not entirely clear how this graphic transcription of the notion of "feedback" will improve our lives or ability to learn, the book is indeed built around

recursive patterns whose syntax is continuously altered. Images spill over from page to page and recto to verso (pp. 1–3, 13a–14a, 159b–156b, 68b–67b, 64b–62b, 58b–57b). They are placed in **mirror relationships**: for instance, the same photo of Tiny Tim appears on the recto of 169b (in green, flipped) and the verso of 170a (BW, upright), only to get picked up again on page 33b. In each case, the accompanying text (in white type) is unrelated: a quote from Pat Nixon on White House dinners (p. 170a), the astrophysicist A. G. W. Cameron ruminating on pulsars (p. 169b), a mariners' maxim (p. 33b). Which isn't to say that Tiny Tim doesn't get quoted as well: on pages 109a ("We were really poor...") and 60b ("I have a lot of respect for the printed word") he does, but in dislocated fashion with respect to the photographs.

Visual doublings and puns abound and are often echoed by the text. The large double *H*'s on the upper left-hand corner of 172a (**H**ippies, t**H**at) recur on the bottom right-hand corner (**H**eaven), with the corner-to-corner graphic effect being equally strong whether one is reading right-side up or upside down. When one reaches the end of page 192a, a cartoon awaits that shows a king speaking to a queen in front of a page (in the sense of courtier) roasting on a spit. "Will you turn the page, dear?" reads the caption when, in point of fact, here the notion of turning involves rotating the book (rather than paging forward). Where Fuller contests the conventional physical notions of "up" and "down" (p. 179a), the page design is reshuffled with the accompanying photograph of a geodesic dome inverted so as to create an unexpected realignment of the upper and lower portions of the page.

While *I Seem to Be a Verb* falls short as a conventional "comprehensive contraction" of Fuller's writing, it succeeds in reinventing **the mass-market paperback as a testbed for nonlinear forms of reading**. One simply cannot "read" *I Seem to Be a Verb* front to back or at a uniform pace. The active engagement of eyes and hands and, for that matter, the mind is required to put together the puzzle, to dip in and out of the dense layerings of data, to connect the dots, to derive pleasure and knowledge from the many *dérives*.

Might this *process*-centered understanding of the book not be a plausible, even compelling, interpretation of Fuller's own adages about knowledge as process (rather than product)?

— I am not a thing—a noun. I seem to be a verb, an evolutionary process—an integral function of the universe. (p. 1)
— I could see only large patterns, houses, trees, and outlines of people...
— Man is a complex of patterns, or processes.
— Whenever I draw a circle, I immediately want to step out of it.
— Life is regenerative and conformity meaningless.
— Bite your tongue. Get a cinder in your eye. When you feel good, you feel nothing.

```
Dear Mr. Schnapp: I am three and
one-half years old. You're right.

[name withheld at the
parents' request]
Champlain, New York
```

Perhaps it is. Fuller appears to have thought so, at least to the extent that he warmly welcomed the book. There were several face-to-face meetings during its preparation. But the paucity of archival traces suggests that Fuller's attitude was more "hands-off" than McLuhan. Fiore, for one, found the partnership less congenial: "The relationship was not as admiring on my part nor as exciting. Perhaps because he had an [arid] turn of mind."[101] Aside from signing off on the concept and approving the finalized product, Fuller's main role appears to have been promotional: he attended the American Booksellers Association convention in June 1970 and integrated promotion of the book into his ever intense lecturing schedule.

Breaking

Is Hard

solos

Fiore and Agel must have been distracted during preparations for the release of *I Seem to Be a Verb* due to two other books published in April 1970: Jerry Rubin's *Do It!*, designed by Fiore, and *The Making of Kubrick's 2001*, edited by Agel. A comparative look at these solo outings may be revealing as regards to what each contributed to the forging of the electric information age book genre.

zippity dada

Do It! is the more refined of the two. It is divided into forty-three short chapters, each of which receives consistent typographical treatment, framed between two double-page cartoon-collages by Spain, titled *Fuck Amerika!* and *Apocalypse*. The book's overall tempo is measured, even though its pages are animated by **a mix of counterculture cartoon strips and photographs** (maximum one or two per page), plus local typographical variations that include one S-shaped layout, cartoon noises (honk, zap, boom), various oversized headlines (a few flipped), and **surrealist-inspired arrangements of smiles, faces, political buttons**, and the like. There are only a few special effects: a clenched fist that punches its way across two pages; a nude girl whose image crosses over between two separate folios; the same cluster of demonstrators who march across the bottom of five pages in a row. The result is a playful, irreverent, highly readable book that combines comic and documentary elements. It has an index, a standard title page, a clear beginning and end.

The book was a collaborative undertaking with Fiore overseeing the design, Jim Retherford "yipping" it (i.e., ghostwriting, producing, and working at Fiore's side), and Rubin's girlfriend Nancy Kurshan "zapping" it (i.e., doing the legwork). Retherford's idea was that the book should "look and feel like the six-o'clock news."[102]

Scenarios of the Revolution

DO iT!

Jerry Rubin

Introduction by
ELDRIDGE CLEAVER

$1.25

10: We Are All Human Be-ins

One day some Berkeley radicals were invited over to the Buddhist temple of some San Francisco hippies. We got high and decided to get the tribes of Haight-Ashbury and Berkeley together.

A Gathering of the Tribes. Golden Gate Park. Free music by all of the rock bands in the city.

The hippies were calling it a Human "Be-in."

Nobody knew what the fuck a Be-in was.

We got stoned on some outasight grass. One Berkeley radical asked: "What are going to be the demands of this demonstration?"

The hippies patiently explained to him that it wasn't a "demonstration" and that we were just going to *be* there.

"People will turn each other on."

"Only good vibes."

"But no demands."

The Berkeley radical kept demanding that there be demands. So somebody gave him a pencil and paper and told him to write some.

It got to be so heavy that one S.F. hippie jumped up and said, "There's got to be more love in this room: *Roll some more joints.*"

People in the streets knew something was up. They seemed to catch on right away. If it had been a political demonstration they would have asked, "What are the issues? What are the demands? Why should we go?"

But this time everybody knew.

The purpose was just to *be.*

Golden Gate Park:
Rock music.
Grass.
Sun. Beautiful bodies.
Paint.
Ecstasy. Rainbows. No strangers!
Everybody smiling. *No picket signs or political banners.*

Our nakedness was our picket sign.

We played out our fantasies like children. We were kids playing "grown-up games." You can be whatever you want to be when you're a kid.

We were cowboys and Indians, pirates, kings, gypsies and Greeks. It was a panorama of history.

The rock bands created a tribal, animal energy.

We were a religion, a family, a culture, with our own music, our own dress, our own human relationships, our own stimulants, our own media.

And we believed that our energy would *turn on the world.*

55

Two hundred of the bravest young men and women in the land, using their North Vietnamese flagpoles as clubs, broke through one line of soldiers and forced their way inside the building, *inside the Pentagon*. The U.S. Army could not keep peace demonstrators out of the Pentagon! The Pentagon was not invincible!

Rifle butts drove us back, twenty skulls cracked and blood flowing.

The demonstrators linked arms while the troops tried to club us away. "Hold that line! Hold that line!" We held and the Army stopped. The Army withdrew, accepting the line which we had won.

Victory!

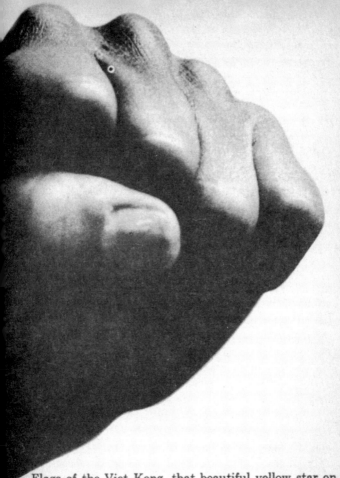

Flags of the Viet Kong, that beautiful yellow star on
a red and blue field, waved high in front of the Pentagon!

Demonstrators snatched helmets from soldiers and ran
back into liberated zones shouting, "Souvenir! A souvenir!"
Beautiful naked chicks went up to GI's and suggested
that they take off their uniforms and come home with them.
Super Joel put a flower in the nozzle of one soldier's
rifle.

i need my space

The Making of Kubrick's 2001 is yet another febrile Agel experiment and is far more content-rich than *Do It!* As Vincent Canby put it in his review in the *New York Times*:

> In some ways the book is as chaotic…and as terribly precious as the McLuhan-Fiore *The Medium Is the Massage*, which Agel "edited and coordinated." However, everything about the book, including the section devoted to reviews and re-reviews, communicates a sense of the film's excitement and of the excitement of movie-making as a sometimes baffling, sometimes inspired, sometimes drearily methodical process of collective creation.[103]

Like its "terribly precious" predecessor, *The Making of Kubrick's 2001* was born on the pages of *Books*: literally so inasmuch as an interview reprinted on page 285 came from the April 1968 issue; other fragments are anticipated in subsequent issues. It has neither an index nor a table of contents nor a conventional set of chapter units, and the chapter "titles" are random quotations from the film script in no way descriptive of what they introduce. Only the running headers offer the reader any reliable guidance.

In the absence of a conventional beginning and end, the book plays. It opens with a quote from the script ("see you on the way back"), next comes the transcript of an entire scene ("Dave. Stop. Stop. Will you. Stop, Dave…."), then the book's title. It concludes with a stream of assertions of pleasurable puzzlement, starting with "Of course I saw *2001: A Space Odyssey*—but now I'm not so sure I did," attributed to the "proofreader of this book" (Agel himself) and ending with a final passage from the script: "Its origin and purpose still a total mystery."

In between these bookends—

THE MAKING OF
KUBRICK'S 2001
EDITED BY JEROME AGEL
96-PAGE PHOTO INSERT

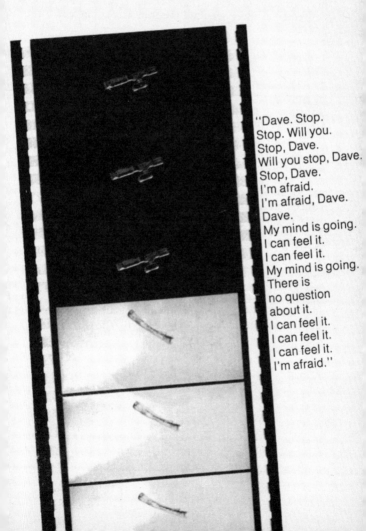

"Dave. Stop.
Stop. Will you.
Stop, Dave.
Will you stop, Dave.
Stop, Dave.
I'm afraid.
I'm afraid, Dave.
Dave.
My mind is going.
I can feel it.
I can feel it.
My mind is going.
There is
no question
about it.
I can feel it.
I can feel it.
I can feel it.
I'm afraid."

fused and puzzled over the difficulty and lack of understanding that was being reported."

Nineteen minutes were trimmed from the original print. Sequences trimmed were Dawn of Man, Orion, Poole exercising in the centrifuge, and Poole's pod exiting from Discovery. Trimming commenced at four P.M. on April 5, 1968, and the first session did not end until seven A.M. the next day. Work continued at this pace until the trim was completed three days later.

Kubrick has talked on three different occasions about the cuts:

1. "*2001* was not the first picture I have tightened after a couple of previews. *Doctor Strangelove* lost an entire pie-throwing sequence at the end because it seemed excessive, and *Paths of Glory* was trimmed between preview and release."

2. "I made all the cuts in *2001* and at no one's request. I had not had an opportunity to see the film complete with music, sound effects, etc., until about a week before it opened, and it does take a few runnings to decide finally how long things should be, especially scenes which do not have narrative advancement as their guideline. Most of the scenes that were cut were impressions of things and could have been anywhere from four times shorter than they were—or four times longer, depending on how you felt about it."

3. "I just felt as I looked at it and looked at it that I could see places all the way through where I could tighten up, and I took out 19 minutes. I don't believe that the trims made a crucial difference. I think it just affected some marginal people. The people who like it, like it no matter what its length, and the same holds true for the people who hate it."

"I must say you guys have come up with something."

Dear Mr. Kubrick:

I am three and one-half years old.
You're right!

[Name withheld on parents' request]
Champlain, New York

Your film was really great. . . . The real reason for sending this letter is to ask for posters for my bedroom walls. . . . I have a film projector if you have any scenes you didn't use.

P.L. Amodio
Kent, England

YOU MADE ME DREAM EYES WIDE OPEN STOP YOURS IS MUCH MORE THAN AN EXTRAORDINARY FILM THANK YOU
FRANCO ZEFFIRELLI
ROME

I am enclosing my four ticket stubs. I would like my money returned, if for no other reason than as an apology for boring the life out of my family and myself for three hours. When will you learn what the public, that you are always screaming about, has known for years. You cannot cover up mediocrity with obscurity.

Mrs. Patricia Attard
Denver

P.S. The tickets were $2.50 each.

my pupils are still dilated, and my breathing sounds like your soundtrack. I don't know if this poor brain will survive another work of the magnitude of *2001*, but it will die (perhaps more accurately "go nova") happily if given the opportunity. Whenever anybody asks me for a description of the movie, I tell them that it is, in sequential order: Anthropological, camp, McLuhan, cybernetic, psychedelic, religious. That shakes them up a lot.

Lots of killings:

> 2 apes
> 1 zebra
> Miscellaneous tapirs
> 3 hibernating astronauts
> 1 H. A. L. 9000
> Poole
> Bowman (reborn)
> Kubrick? ("I never discuss money,
> but I own a good piece of it.")

Lots of little films:

> Computer readouts
> Welcome of the Voiceprint girl
> Japanese wrestling
> Aries landing at Clavius
> Love scene in automobile
> BBC "World Tonight"
> Conferences with mission control
> Dr. Floyd's final report detailing truth
>   about the mission
> Dr. Floyd's daughter on Picturephone
> Birthday greeting to Poole

Lots of snapshots:

> I.D. badges
> News photographer in the moon conference room
> Group picture in the TMA-1 pit.

•

Error in 2001:

Heywood Floyd's lunch is sipped; what he doesn't sip then slides down his straw. It should have stayed in the straw in the zero gravity of space.

•

Mission Commander Dave Bowman makes it to a room best described as:

"Louis Quinze" — Peter Dibble, *Women's Wear Daily*

"Brilliantly-lit Louis Seize" — Bruce Gillespie, *Australian Science Fiction Review*

"Louis XVI hotel suite" — Joseph Morgenstern, *Newsweek*

"Period French bedroom" — B. L. Drew, *Camden* (N. J.) *Courier Post*

"Strange Colonial room" — G. Youngblood, *Los Angeles Free Press*

"Room decorated in a modified Empire style" — G. Curner, *Australian Science Fiction Review*

"18th century hotel-room-like" — Judith Crist, *New York* magazine

"Magnificent marble palazzo" — S. Johnson, *Montreal Star*

"Startlingly conventional room, which seems to exist independently of time and space" — *T&D*, San Diego, Calif.

"Miami Beach hotel elegance" — G. Bourke, *Miami Herald*

Headlines over *2001* reviews and articles read like found poetry!

> It may sound like Vienna, but it's outer space
> A machine for all seasons
> A superb wreck
> Lost in the stars
> Space for the tyro
> Future tense, present tensions
> Escaping into orbit
> Stanley Kubrick, please come down
> Kubrick, farther out
> Up, up and away
> After man
> Is Stanley Kubrick Dr. Strange?

—a rich mix of materials is laid out in clusters.
The mix includes:

— **a witty pseudointroduction** that starts by pointing
out that the cost of building the Hale telescope
atop Mount Palomar was the same as that of making
the film (p. 10)
— that then splices together quotes from the likes
of Bob Dylan, André Breton, Wyndham Lewis, and
Leonard Cohen with ludic details about Agel's
own experience of the film ("I have seen Stanley
Kubrick's musical comedy every day since it opened
in Manhattan nearly two years ago, and I can hardly
wait to see it today"), factoids about the film ("'Hush'
was the key word during production"), and aphorisms ("We are all machines. [What happened to
your lunch?]"; "We have met the enemy and we are
theirs.") (p. 12)
— and that concludes with a surreal query: "Have you
looked at your air conditioner?" (p. 13)

— **an anthology** of source materials made up of
— Arthur C. Clarke's short story "The Sentinel," on
which the film is based (p. 15)
— the transcripts of interviews with experts on
space and astronomy that Kubrick filmed for an
intended ten-minute prologue (that was eventually
cut) (p. 27–57)
— Jeremy Bernstein's profile of Kubrick from the
New Yorker (p. 58)
— **a ninety-six-page photo insert** alternating between
sequences of frames and stills that document the
behind-the-scenes work on the film, accompanied
by a collage-style commentary (pp. 73–164)
— **audience responses** that run the gamut from
demands for reimbursement of the cost of tickets

("I would like my money returned, if for no other reason than as an apology for boring the life out of my family and myself for three hours") to Freudian and Jungian decodings of the film to celebratory poems. Statements by Franco Zeffirelli and Federico Fellini are patched into the mix. In some cases, "Kubrick" responds to the audience letters. (pp. 171–92)

— all of the major reviews of the film as well as "re-reviews"—reviews based on second viewings— and reviews of the novel and soundtrack (pp. 206–55)

— a miscellany that includes technical details about the film and its script, *2001* trivia, the promotional campaign for the film and its protagonists, the awards that it won and was denied, plus interviews, interviews, interviews. (pp. 321–27) Among them:
— Kubrick's 1968 lengthy and detailed *Playboy* interview (pp. 328–54)
— but also an interview with *Books*, at the end of which the director agreed only to the publication of four short comments. Agel went ahead and published the "interview" in the following format, reproduced in the book—

We've just spent eight hours interviewing Stanley Kubrick.
We've just spent eight hours interviewing Stanley Kubrick.
"I'd rather not discuss the film."
We've just spent eight hours interviewing Stanley Kubrick.
We've just spent eight hours interviewing Stanley Kubrick.
"It takes about a year to let an idea reach an obsessional state so I know what I really want to do with it."
We've just spent eight hours interviewing Stanley Kubrick.
We've just spent eight hours interviewing Stanley Kubrick.
We've just spent eight hours interviewing Stanley Kubrick.
We've just spent eight hours interviewing Stanley Kubrick.
We've just spent eight hours interviewing Stanley Kubrick.
We've just spent eight hours interviewing Stanley Kubrick.
We've just spent eight hours interviewing Stanley Kubrick.
We've just spent eight hours interviewing Stanley Kubrick.
We've just spent eight hours interviewing Stanley Kubrick.
"The feel of the experience is the important thing, not the ability to verbalize or analyze it."
We've just spent eight hours interviewing Stanley Kubrick.
We've just spent eight hours interviewing Stanley Kubrick.
We've just spent eight hours interviewing Stanley Kubrick.
We've just spent eight hours interviewing Stanley Kubrick.
We've just spent eight hours interviewing Stanley Kubrick.
We've just spent eight hours interviewing Stanley Kubrick.
We've just spent eight hours interviewing Stanley Kubrick.
We've just spent eight hours interviewing Stanley Kubrick.
We've just spent eight hours interviewing Stanley Kubrick.
We've just spent eight hours interviewing Stanley Kubrick.
We've just spent eight hours interviewing Stanley Kubrick.
"You have to be prepared to make adjustments."
We've just spent eight hours interviewing Stanley Kubrick.
We've just spent eight hours interviewing Stanley Kubrick.

The resulting volume is controlled chaos with a purpose. It provides at once an invaluable point of entry to *2001: A Space Odyssey*—"absolutely essential," in the words of one reviewer in *Film Quarterly*—and a performative hybrid with attributes of the film monograph, the fanzine, the technical report, the album, the gossip column, the magazine write-up, a game of Trivial Pursuit...all for the price of one.[104]

...and how!

The formula worked. The book sold well and so did *Do It!*
The first rode on the coattails of *2001*'s achievement of
cult-movie status; the second on the wave of media attention to the trial of the Chicago Seven.

What did Fiore do after *Do It!*?…increasingly traditional design and typographical work, taking on a long
series of jobs with the Franklin Library that would encompass the design of chapter medallions, maps, and drawings for mid-1970s editions of such classics as *Tales from
the Arabian Nights*, the plays of Euripides, and the Robert
Fitzgerald translation of Homer's *Iliad* and *Odyssey*.

What did Agel make after *The Making of 2001: A
Space Odyssey*?…Additional odysseys into the future.
Futurology became the stock and trade of the final run
of INVENTORY BOOKS. These cover the full spectrum of
possibilities already codified in the prior collaborations,
from the visually driven (*The Medium Is the Massage*) to
the text-driven (*War and Peace in the Global Village*) to the
quotation-driven (*I Seem to Be a Verb*). A few new weapons, borrowed from the Kubrick book and the *Whole Earth
Catalog*, enter the Agel arsenal: reader polls, anthologies
of letters and expert interviews, out-of-left-field lists, list-
ings of resources, appeals to do-it-yourself. The books
continue to be composed out of the same box of clippings
and quotations, so there are recurrences and slippages
from one book to the next.

**AN INVENTORY WOULD LOOK SOMETHING LIKE
THE FOLLOWING—**

Is Today Tomorrow?
A Synergistic Collage of Alternative Futures
Jerome Agel
1972

the genre blender
Love at first sight between a quotation mosaic and a
school curriculum on futurology.

recyclings
There are several from *War and Peace in the Global Village*
and *I Seem to be Verb*, among them details from Bosch's
Garden of Earthly Delights; the spiderweb on pages **72–73**
and Buster Keaton hanging from a clock hand on page **85**.
On page **126**, a note addressed to Kubrick in *The Making
of 2001* resurfaces as if addressed to Agel:

```
Dear Mr. Agel: I am three and
one-half years old. You're right.
```

antipasti?
The futurist Herman Kahn makes a cameo appearance on
pages **12–13**. (Agel was no ideologue; he was interested in
influential thinkers, whether of the left or of the right).

self-references
The four photographs on the lead page are of Agel's
daughter Julie; the Mickey Mouse alarm clock on page **87**
sat atop Agel's desk faithfully delivering the *first humilia-
tion of the day*.

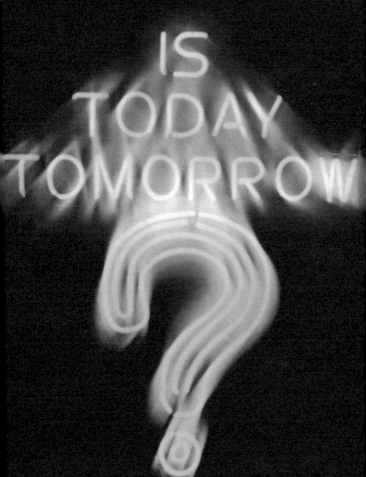

IS TODAY TOMORROW

A Synergistic Collage of Alternative Futures

JEROME AGEL

Technically, We Are

Beyond Survival

"The image of economic man still dominates most of our control institutions and constrains our possible solutions to large-scale problems within its bounds. To a great extent, it is already a built-in and unexamined premise for many of the refined methodological approaches to futures forecasting, and it operates as the latent criterion for evaluating the forward dispositions of energies and technologies for societal use." --
John McHale

"It's still the same old story, a fight for love and glory."

From reactionary to "welfare" socialist, policies are built around survival. Ours is only the success of squirrels in autumn —but how many acorns can we stash away?

LIFE IMPRISONED BY THE DEAD HAND OF ECONOMY.

If old people show the same desires, the same feelings and the same requirements as the young, the world looks upon them with disgust...the fact that for the last 15 or 20 years of his life a man should be no more than a reject, a piece of scrap, reveals the failure of our civilization... [it is] by concentrating one's efforts upon the fate of the most unfortunate, the worst used of all, that one can successfully shake a society to its foundations." -- Simone de Beauvoir

Kurt Vonnegut: "What is not realized is that one doesn't learn in one semester what he has to know. The flower blooms at 40."

FLASH: Human urine can be used as the electrolyte in wet cell batteries. Old or failing batteries can be recharged any time you have to go—literally.

among the cited
René Dubos, Eugene Zamiatin, Alan Watts, Fyodor Dostoyevsky, Lewis Mumford, Guy Debord, Tristan Tzara, Ivan Illich, Claude Levi-Strauss, André Breton, John McHale. (Yes, *the* Guy Debord.)

tttoons
Nearly all the book's illustrations were drawn by Milton Harris, a regular contributor to *Books*; a strip from *Peanuts* plus a *New Yorker* cartoon by Frank Modell are thrown in for good measure.

artistes
Only the trusty Hieronymus Bosch makes the cut.

finding aids
Surely you weren't expecting something as jejune as a table of contents or an index? Pagination and running headers remain scattershot until the final section (pp. **129–92**). Cast in the same mold of *A funny thing happened on the way to the future* and *Cut them off at the past*, the titles play hide and seek (with an emphasis on the HIDE).

mnemonic in chief?
The color cover photograph of flashing neon sign with the words of the title followed by a question mark recurs on the back reversed, in black and white, with the sign switched off.

juice
LIST- and POLL-like. Pages **33–57** feature a suite of surreal inventories bearing titles like *So what else is new?*,
Thursdays off for thinking, *TV from Mars*, *Pornotopia*,
Grokking, *Tachyons*, and *1000-Seat Planes*. Between
pages **129–69** one hundred experts answer the question
"do *you* believe that young people can handle curricula on
the future?" Answer: *affirmative*.

invitations to groan
"Lobotomies are back. All hail the psychothe*Rapist*"; "the
point past which democracy becomes demockery"; the
university is a "Concentration Campus."

alphas and omegas
A = the first page reads: "The next 73.9 years are already
here. Hi!"

Ω = the final page shows a full-page photograph of
a woman being hit in face with a pie. Pieing is how you
translate *Massage*'s "Good morning!" and "300 m.p.h.
wind bail-out experiment conducted by the US Navy" into
tomorrowese.

Herman Kahnsciousness:
The Megaton Ideas of the One-Man Think Tank
Produced by Jerome Agel
1973

the genre blender
A text-driven mosaic of the thoughts of the founder of
the conservative Hudson Institute with the ragged feel
of a counterculture rag. The book's throw weight is measured in megatons not because of Kahn's physical heft but
because of his willingness to contemplate winnable scenarios for all-out nuclear war.

recyclings
The title page reuses a June 1966 *Books* cover by Sam
Gross showing an armless female nude being tickled
all over by centipedes; there are also scenes from the
court life of the New York Knicks (cf. *Is Today Tomorrow?*).
On page **151**, a note addressed to Kubrick in *The Making
of 2001*, re-addressed to Agel in *Is Today Tomorrow?*,
resurfaces as—

> Dear Mr. Kahn: I am three and
> one-half years old. You're right.

antipasti?
An allusion to extraterrestrial life on page **163** is cred-
ited to Carl Sagan, Agel's collaborator on the next two
INVENTORY BOOKS. Their subject? Extraterrestrial life.
Kahn was a true believer in the glowing prospects for the
colonization of space.

A SIGNET NON-FICTION • W5361 • $1.50

The Megaton Ideas
of the One-Man Think Tank

HERMAN KAHNSCIOUSNESS

Produced by
JEROME AGEL

"Herman Kahn's work exemplifies how much power the
relevant ideas of a great mind can actually exercise over
the affairs and thoughts of men; radical jumps in the mind
precede the revolutions in society."—*The New York Times.*

'Stick 'em up'

accidental (or whoops) plunge into the holocaust.

just because a button is pressed and a little old bomb wipes out out out gone, the rest of the world really doesn't have to commit suicide.

self-references
After a quote on page **35** from Agel's own *A World without...What Our Presidents Didn't Know* come treasures from the family vault: a photograph taken by Agel's daughter is printed on pages **58–59**; and she is also present as a little girl among the birches on page **127**. On page **136** her Howdy Doody doll appears in a photographic effigy. (It is described as a loan from the "Julie Agel collection" and was deaccessioned in the 1980s.)

among the cited
In this solo Kahn-Kahn by the one-man megaton think-tank there's room for little more-than-passing mentions of other *auctores*.

tttoons
Milton Harris is again the book's main illustrator; three other cartoons derive from the *New Yorker* (Robert Kraus, William Steig, Robert Day), plus one each from the *Saturday Review* and *Industrial Worker* (1939).

artistes
Trains smashing through walls and mantelpieces...*merçi Monsieur Magritte!*

finding aids
No table of contents, no pagination, no running headers, no titles. What, me worry?

mnemonic in chief?
It's Fashion Week on the Hudson. Beauty queens sprint across the cosmos, Soviet Premier Alexei Kosygin wears an Indian chieftain's feather headdress ("Keep Kool with Kosygin"); a working-class lug sports a Jizz Inc. TITS t-shirt (*nomina sunt consequentia rerum*).

juice

A photo-novella on pages **30–33** documents the weekly visit of the official neighborhood burglar to a middle-class home ("See you next Thursday!" he says politely as he departs). But for higher forms of wisdom, it's best to consult HK: "If you are trying to find the direction of the flow of a river, you can't examine it with a microscope. You have to stand back—way back. Maybe 1000 years back" (p. **169**).

invitations to groan

Wargasm; tab,000,000 (= TABOO...BOO...BOO); "force, like skin, is a permanent element in society—and, like skin, it can break out in a rash moment." Smileys abound. They keep the guillotine company and set over the horizon like the sun.

alphas and omegas

A = a hand reaching down across the page toward a joke: "Two Jewish businessmen, who don't trust each other, live in a little Polish town between Minsk and Pinsk. In the wee wee hours of a morning, they chance to meet at the railroad station. "And where are you going, my dear friend?" "To Minsk." "You lie! You *are* going to Minsk."

Ω = a cartoon by Robert Day from the *New Yorker* in which a dad is changing a flat in the rain with his children peering out impatiently from within the car. He explains: "This is *life*, this is what is happening. We *can't* switch to another channel."

Other Worlds
Carl Sagan
Produced by Jerome Agel
1975

the genre blender
The visually driven INVENTORY BOOK strikes back. After
The Cosmic Connection, which was a text-driven and
pun-free hardcover firmly under the control of Celestial
Steersman Sagan, Agel's once again back at the helm.

recyclings
"It is [STILL] the business of the future to be dangerous"
on page **135**; Bosch bashes his way back onto page **72**.

antipasti
None (saving room for dessert).

self-references
No family photos?! Is the producer asleep at the wheel?

among the cited
James Elroy Flecker, Albert Einstein, William Shakespeare,
Horace, Leonardo da Vinci, Diane Ackerman × 10, Alfred
Lord Tennyson, Gerard Manley Hopkins, Thomas
Carlyle, H. G. Wells, Matthew Arnold, John Donne, John
Bunyan, William Blake...The last word(s) go(es) to Nikos
Kazantzakis.

Y6439 ★ $1.95 ★ A BANTAM BOOK

Is there life out there?

"Our first steps into space have already shown us other worlds far stranger than anything in science fiction."

Other Worlds

by Carl Sagan

Author of
The Cosmic Connection

Produced by
Jerome Agel

At an instant some 15-billion years ago, the cosmic clock began to tick—and the Universe, or at least its present incarnation, was born.

For some 10-billion years the clock ticked away. And then our Sun turned on, the planets formed, life and intelligence evolved.

We know the beginning of this story but not the end.

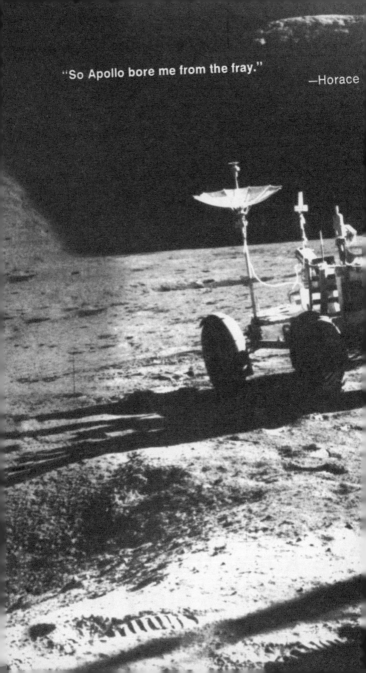

"So Apollo bore me from the fray."

—Horace

What a pity that our nearest neighbor is so dull. But a person who has never seen another will find even a dull neighbor interesting.

tttoons
A platoon's worth—the *New Yorker* (Robert Grossman, Alan Dunn × 2, Chas Addams × 2, Charles Sauers); Orlando Busino × 2; *Playboy* (Gahan Wilson, John Dempsey); *Punch* (Lawrence Siggs); *Grin and Bear It* (George Lichty); a bit of Grandville; a Charlie Brown strip; with multiple pages from George Locke's anthology of pre-WWI British sci-fi illustration; and *Worlds Apart* (pp. **50–58**) as a chaser.

artiste
Vincent Van Gogh, have you looked at your air conditioner?

finding aids
Sporadically paginated. The pace is contemplative. No need to deploy the emergency chute.

mnemonic in chief?
Pattern overlays (nebulae, starry night, H-Alpha solar radiation, aerial view of farmland, overhead photo of Manhattan skyline, more nebulae); *la page blanche* (pp. **66–67**) with the legend in 4-point type: "Space is nice. And it's pretty empty." Blurry space porn redux.

juice
"Predicting the future is tough." (Carl Sagan is as tough as they come).

invitations to groan
Horace sings "Apollo bore me from the fray" over the Apollo lunar lander, "Better Red Than Dead" refers to Mars, and there is talk of a certain Johnny Starseed. Alpha Centauri apples, anyone?

alphas and omegas
A = "I cannot say I believe that there is life out there. But it is possible" (cautious first words).

Ω = "either we will be stupid and destroy ourselves or we will be wise" (premonitory last words) followed by a cartoon of Noah's Space Ark.

It's About Time & It's About Time
Alan Lakein
Produced by Jerome Agel
1975

the genre blender
The massage to beat all massages.

recyclings
On the title page, the Mickey Mouse clock hovers over
Stonehenge. The Knicks are back in the knick of time six
pages later. So are: the Sinclair Oil dinosaur (from *I Seem
to Be a Verb*), Sagan's Pioneer 10 plaque for extraterres-
trials ("Streaking Buffs"), and Field Marshall McLuhan's
ALLATONCENESS. On page **156**, a note first addressed
to Kubrick in *The Making of 2001*, re-addressed to Agel in
Is Today Tomorrow?, re-re-addressed to Kahn in *Herman
Kahnsciousness*, returns as—

> Dear Mr. Lakein: I am three and
> one-half years old. You're right.

(All three are right.)

antipasti
The prior pitch to **you**, **your neighborhood**, **your world**
takes a definitive swerve here in the direction of Agel's
next avocation: self-help and "curious fact" books.

self-references
Twelve-year-old Jesse Agel has his say ("Time goes by so
fast when you're having fun").

B7647 ★ $2.25 A BANTAM BOOK

IT'S ABOUT TIME
& IT'S ABOUT TIME

BY ALAN LAKEIN
PRODUCED BY JEROME AGEL

Take phone calls only at specified hours.

Don't wait in a gasoline line unless you've got a car.

Don't open junk mail or letters if your address is stenciled.

Read only the first line of every paragraph.

SET PRIORITIES

Don't feel a need to catch up.

Delegate.

Don't waste others' time.

Say "no."

Live above a supermarket.

Catch up on your sleep.

Play the LP instead of trekking to the concert.

Run down and up escalators.

Don't eat anchovies.

Combine office and home.

Learn how long it takes to get to the point where you know what you're talking about.

Live and work on the ground floor.

Have associates stand during meetings.

Do deep knee bends while brushing teeth.

Listen to something while shaving and bathing.

Accept calls from no one except the President of the U.S. and your spouse (and they should know better).

Fire the incompetent.

Fire everyone.

YA

WN

among the cited
William Blake, Anne Frank, Rudyard Kipling, Mopsy Kennedy, Heraclitus, Alexander Solzhenitsyn, Virginia Woolf, Goethe, Charles Mingus (with discography), Eugene Ionesco, and Emily Dickinson.

tttoons
New Yorker, *New Yorker* what a wonderful source! (Donald Reilly, Mischa Richter, Richard Taylor, Chon Day, Alan Dunn, James Stevenson are all there, plus a *New Yorker* cover.) A *Chicago* (*Daily News*) interloper interlopes on pages **148–49**.

artistes
Juan Genovés, M. C. Escher, Marcel Duchamp. (Yes, *the* Marcel Duchamp.)

finding aids
It's about time for **you** to follow **your own nose** (and the occasional page marker). Don't even ask about the rest: an apparatus is a waste of time.

mnemonic in chief?
ENTROPY yawns across pages **37–39**; YAWNS entropize pages **114–15**. The book's central question is posed on pages **46–47**: "What is the best use of your time right now?" The answer comes two pages later, courtesy of the Hero-Boy Restaurant, in the form of the world's first four-page-long submarine sandwich. This Big Boy, tagged "FAST!," returns at the book's conclusion under the title "The Living End." (Time for seconds!)

juice
a scattering of times (Spring, Monday, Tuesday, Noon, Fall); a smattering of lists (priorities, quotes on death, Big Time).

invitations to groan

"getting Shakespeare to change *Hamlet's* opening line hasn't a ghost of a chance"; "don't be gulled" (p. **81**) in the company of photographic seagulls; "we live off the fatuousness of the land"; "Dick Caveatt Emptor."

alphas and omegas

A = *Spring* on the lead page = a suicidal fall through the void (full-page photo)

Ω = *Time Will Tell* on the last page = an apple with an arrow shot through it means +/- that Time will tell William Tell; or William Tell will tell time; or William Time will tell Tell.

&c.

The inventory above is incomplete because, from the start, **Agel's understanding of book "production" was fluid**. It encompassed everything from typophotographic hybrids like the above to more conventional projects where he assumed some combination of the roles of agent, coauthor, editor, producer, and packager. Among the latter are anthologies documenting the work of the Radical Therapist collective, a collaboration with the British psychiatrist Humphry Osmond, a self-authored experiment in speculative history titled *A World without...What Our Presidents Didn't Know*, and the sorts of diet, self-help, trivia, and historical fact books that would become his meal ticket during subsequent decades.[105]

However diverse, this corpus of nonphototypo-graphical works shares the same emphasis on the **activation of the reader that operates at the perceptual/organizational level** in the INVENTORY BOOKS. Either in conventional linear fashion or through thickly layered verbal-visual pop-flavored sandwiches, all communicate some version of the following script to the reader: even if this book is "by" a major thinker, you fill in the blanks, you connect the dots, you navigate the book forward or backward to find the tasty tidbits; look for the patterns, ideas, and story line yourself.[106] They tender the promise that, if you follow these instructions, in return, you will discover that not only is this a book about you, your neighborhood, your job, your government, your world, but also about how to make them yours.

u turns

There is a strand of this empowerment narrative that has deep roots in the American traditions of self-help, individualism, and pragmatism: models that migrated from the moral to the commercial realm during the nineteenth and twentieth centuries, becoming defining features of the mass cultural vernacular of advertising. Through the electric information age book, this strand becomes interwoven with another strand, of avant-gardist extraction, that explores nonlinear, reader-centered models of culture and communication both to disrupt conventional norms and to forge models of selfhood, society, and art practice, aligned with the needs of the eras of industry and information. The dream that these two branches of modernity might merge and forge **AN AVANT-GARDE MASS CULTURE** at once haunted and tantalized the historical avant-gardes, constrained to operate within the restricted circle of the laboratory.

Futurism illustrates the predicament well (eluded only partly even by successors such as the Bauhaus and constructivism). The movement was born on the front page of a daily newspaper. It modeled its revolution in poetic language on the mass communications technologies of its era. Its arsenal of cultural-political tactics was directly drawn from contemporary models of mass agitation and promotion. Yet, much like Gabriele D'Annunzio, its nemesis and idol, it defended the autonomy of art with tenacity even as it sought out mass media and a mass audience. Futurism's founder, F. T. Marinetti, could simply not conceive of experimental art as commerce or of commerce as a cultural experiment. Every futurist publishing house was a money-loser by design. The patronage model remained the traditional one of a wealthy patron—Marinetti himself, the Marchesa Casati, even Benito Mussolini—bankrolling an art ultimately understood as holy excess, excrement, *dépense*.

Half a century later, the electric information age book comes along, ushered in by cybernetics, television, the paperback revolution, the counterculture, and, especially, pop art. The phantasmagoria of commodities with its animated world of mascots, slogans, jingles, logos, and narratives of transformation about you is now enshrined in the Parnassus of contemporary culture from bottom to top, supermarket to museum, classroom to barroom, Tube to page. New mergers of the high and low are the result: **THE BOOK PRODUCER** consorts with the **ENGLISH LIT PROFESSOR** who, once disinclined to admit the commodity gods into the modernist pantheon, is now ready to abandon the Ivory Tower for the glitter and hubbub of the marketplace. Other thinkers, futurists, policy makers, and even scientists are no less eager to join the march toward a future of comprehensive contractions for the Mass Age. (The march will prove relatively short.)

son of *Massage*

Popularizations have never been popular with critics or scholars, all the less so *experimental* popularizations. Agel's late-1960s and early-1970s publishing experiments are no exception. Critical scorn rained down on many, if not most of them, sometimes in bucketfuls, with Agel channeling opprobrium into *Decide for Yourself* campaigns.

Yet in these books what McLuhan called the "mosaic of instantaneous communication" gives rise to a new publishing genre that, for all its period specificity and slapdash graphic-verbal roughness, resonates with some of the defining design challenges of our own era: a hybrid that is "part book, part magazine, part storyboard" and, indeed, part advertisement, populated by cross-media puns; rapid shifts in pace and scale; framings of the book as screen, windshield, lithographic plate, another reader's book.[107] I have tried to suggest that what remains compelling about these experiments is their radicalization of McLuhan's long-stated claim that "my books constitute the process rather than the completed *product* of discovery"; or of Fuller's assertion that knowledge is not a category, thing, or noun but a verb, an evolutionary process."[108] Rarely if ever has the Book been the place where process marries print. But such nuptials are becoming the order of the day in the era of e-publishing, print +, and post-print.

A success or a failure? The answer depends on the parameters one adopts. From the standpoint of sales, Agel's INVENTORY BOOKS were a success, though the market for them was tapering off by the mid-1970s, and a few sold poorly (*Is Today Tomorrow?* and *Herman Kahnsciousness*). In the wake of *The Medium Is the Massage*, the publishing industry rushed to embrace the genre but steered it away from popularizations of major thinkers toward more secure market segments like music, television, and film books. The industry itself underwent massive consolidation during the 1970s and 1980s with the autonomy of individual editors, not to mention of packagers and producers, compromised in the process. This much is certain: to keep the franchise if not aloft, then at least afloat during the mid-1970s, Agel went back to the well time and again. And the well in question bore the name Marshall McLuhan.

As early as January 1973, Agel contacted his former collaborator about updating *The Medium Is the Massage*. McLuhan answered in the affirmative, prompting the following note reply:

> How would you propose to work? Dictate preliminary man-uscript and picture ideas for our re-writing and illustrating in a *Massage* format and style, per your final approval: an approach that worked perfectly when we did the original *Massage*? About 128-page book? You asked how much of the present *Massage* should be retained for liaison? I suggest that the first part of this new work start with the comment, "...AS WE WERE SAYING," with some general remarks about the original *Massage*, updating it, and then all new material. (Quentin will not be involved in this produc-tion. I will be the sole responsible design, production, and contract party, per my recent successes.)[109]

A few months later, the project's contours were mutable as ever:

> A very short book, no more than 64 pages, a summing up and a projection: where your head is at, where you think ours ought to be. You could tape record your basic thoughts that we should have, we would transcribe the material, and I would respond with a few questions for your answering. Except for page one of this proposed book, I propose that no pictures appear. Page one would be the picture from the last page of the *Massage*: an early satellite view of the Moon and the Whitehead quote, "It is the business of the future to be dangerous." Pages two and three would carry the title

AS I WAS SAYING. We could of course incorporate a few illustrations, including some from the *Massage* in counterpoint to new material, but I think a book as I propose above—**A BOOK OF IDEAS!**—would be the best thing you could do with me at this time.[110]

The conversation about what came to be called *Son of Massage* carried on for another five years with iterations of the project that encompassed:

—   a reissue of the original supplemented by the following topics: "Changing American character since TV. The Hologram as reversed perspective. Ecology and the end of Nature. Complementary to *The Medium Is the Massage*: the user is the content (and implications of that). The decline of private identity. Simultaneously, Watergate provides a good paradigm of the new to absolutist ethic for the public sector." (McLuhan's proposal in June 1973)[111]
—   "A history of the future: a *looking backward* to be called *Predicting the Past*—you in the year 2079 looking backward?—or a Q. and A. book, maybe based on your responses to interesting letters? There need not be illustrations." (Agel's proposal in March 1978)[112]

There were detours along the way: preparations for a second edition of *Understanding Media*; the development of a series of sixty-second television programs titled *Keep in Touch with...* for Kaiser Broadcasting "featuring, one at a time, seminal thinkers"; requests on McLuhan's part to strip the Joycean apparatus from all subsequent printings of *War and Peace in the Global Village*; an Agel project on first memories.[113] There were also tokens of skepticism on McLuhan's part: after receiving his copy of *Herman Kahnsciousness*, he wrote back expressing the hope that "we can improve on what passes for *Kahnsciousness!*"[114]

The obstacle that doomed the project from the outset, however, was time: a McLuhan stretched so thin that even a slimmed-down *Son of Massage* would be fated to slim down to nothingness.

Burroughs to Burroughs

The final word must go to Fiore who, alone among the members of the founding triumvirate, set about theorizing their collaborative efforts through a cut-and-paste essay published in the December 1968 issue of the educational review *Media and Methods* (later remixed for *The Future of Time*, coedited by Agel's collaborator Osmond).[115]

"The Future of the Book" begins with a hieroglyph that charts multiple simultaneous futures for publishing, insists that "what is new is new not because it has never been there before, but because it has changed in quality," and forecasts a radical reshaping of publishing in the age of information overload. It then proceeds to examine the great computing/publishing/media mergers of the era, tracks the expanded analytic capacities of mainframe computers like the Burroughs 6500, and documents how the rise of instant communications networks, supported by everything from computer-driven cathode ray tube printers to talking typewriters to long-distance xerography, is restructuring fields of knowledge.

The concluding paste throws the switch from tech to lit, from the Burroughs Corporation to William Burroughs. It consists in a meta cut-and-paste, reproducing a page from a Burroughs scrapbook and an accompanying quotation in which Fiore surely found validation for the vision of knowledge design that has been excavated in the present book: design dedicated to probing "precisely how word and image get around on very, very complex association lines."[116]

The challenge has an invitingly contemporary ring: to craft knowledge that rises to the highest standards of rigor while exploring rich tangles of associative paths.

Let's leave it at that.

Are you sure you have everything that you came in with?

WILLIAM BURROUGHS: "... I've recently done a lot of experiments with scrapbooks. I'll read in the newspaper something that reminds me of, or has relation to, something I've written. I'll cut out the picture or the article and paste it in a scrapbook beside the words from my book ..."

"... I've been interested in precisely how word and image get around on very, very complex association lines."

"Writers at Work"
The Paris Review Interviews
3rd series. Viking, 1967

Case

Studies

INVENTORY BOOKS encompass an array of publishing experiments from the photo- to the textcentric, from the linear to the kaleidoscopic. Since there is little agreement as regards the exact typophotographic genre to which each experiment belongs, a multiplicity of self-designations are adopted: among them, "essays," "documentaries," "magazines," "albums," and "collections." Five genres are examined in the following thumbnail histories:

photo•essayism probes John Berger's influential interweavings of the verbal and photographic essay against the work of McLuhan collaborator, the anthropologist Edmund Carpenter.

album•art surveys books structured like movies or long play recordings.

magazine•book situates the paperback magazines of the late 1960s and early 1970s in relation to the literary digests of the preceding decades.

agit•pop tracks the role performed by pamphlet- or manifesto-books in period protest movements.

shelf•help looks into two iterations of jump-cut solipsism.

photo • essayism

In the same year as the publication of *The Medium Is the Massage*, the first of John Berger's collaborations with the Swiss documentary photographer Jean Mohr appeared with Penguin. Titled **A Fortunate Man**, it interlaced the

A Fortunate Man
John Berger and Jean Mohr / Designed by Jerry Cinamon / London: Allen Lane/ The Penguin Press, 1967.

smooth cadences of Berger's prose with black-and-white photographs of the general practitioner John Sassall at work in rural England. A direct descendant of the James Agee/Walker Evans *Let Us Now Praise Famous Men* school of documentary books, the volume transports its reader to a distant time and place where everyday human actions and gestures take on a gentle grandeur. The tone treads the fine line between the elegiac (here is a fragile, imperiled world) and the humbly heroic (here is a world that is at once human and humane), with the text superimposed over Mohr's photographs only in two opening double-paged spreads that serve as establishing shots. In the rest of the book, as in Berger's successive photo-essays, the arts of photography and narration dance about one another like secret lovers at a dinner party, obliquely eyeing one another but never touching. "In this book what can best be said in images is said that way; what can best be said in words is written," wrote Berger in a brief essay, "Words and Images," published in issue 11 (1966) of Herbert Spencer's *Typographica*. "[T]ogether they make the picture of the man as we both understand him" (p. **47**).

The elusive dance becomes a method in the companion volume to the BBC television series *Ways of Seeing*. Earlier in the same *Typographica* article, Berger had pointed to the desirability of sometimes granting images priority over words:

> No editor yet thinks of a photographic library as a possible *vocabulary*; nobody dares to place images as precisely in  relation to a text as a quotation would be placed; few writers yet think of using pictures to make their argument. In my own limited field of art-criticism, no critic has been allowed to use reproductions as anything but "illustrations": they might be used as diagrams or as *the* content of the article—as the drawings of a strip cartoon are the fundamental content of the strip. (p. **45**)

Ways of Seeing implements the program from the outset. The cover of *A Fortunate Man* had featured Dr.

Ways of Seeing
John Berger with Sven Blomberg, Chris Fox, Michael Dibb, and Richard Hollis / London: BBC and Penguin Books, 1972.

Sassall opening a door so as to imply a direct analogy with the reader opening the book. The cover of *Ways of Seeing* features a window, cited/sited with surgical precision within the flow of Berger's prose, that both opens up a view of the book's insides—it prefigures the layout on pages **7–8**—and obstructs. The window is René Magritte's *Key to Dreams*: an opaque exploration of the match and mismatch between names and nouns. (In the upper left-hand quadrant, a horse's head hovers above the label "the door.")

The cover is indicative with respect to a paperback original that interweaves purely pictorial essays with essays proper in order "to start a process of questioning" (p. **5**). The text—bolded throughout, unhyphenated, printed with an irregular right edge—is spaced so as to emphasize the argumentative role performed by images. Captions are postponed to oblige the reader to embrace reading and looking as cognitive equals. Magazine advertisements are juxtaposed with consecrated masterpieces in ways that betray debts to McLuhan's *Mechanical Bride.* There is even a direct borrowing from page **69** of *The Medium Is the Massage*: Abraham Bosse's *Les Perspecteurs*, a plate from *Manière universelle de M. Desargues pour pratiquer la perspective* (1647), appears (unattributed) on page **17**.

Any overlaps between Berger's critical brand of photo-essayism and the INVENTORY BOOK as interpreted by Agel and Fiore end here. Even if "television, pictorial

journalism, advertising, the need to educate quickly…are changing the balance between word and image" ("Words and Images" [p. **45**]), every medium possesses a distinctive dignity and depth for Berger. As a result, whether he is documenting the lives of ordinary individuals or providing a panoramic (re)vision of the history of art, the photo-essayist makes his arguments through *position and juxtaposition*, not through typophotographical fusions, the alteration of images, or the razzle-dazzle of cuts and pastes. The latter techniques are a two-edged sword. They are both the weapons employed by avant-gardes to demystify contemporary society and the tools of commercial advertising, forever available for purposes of mystification.

A Seventh Man: Migrant Workers in Europe / Written by John Berger / Photographed by Jean Mohr / Designed by Richard Hollis / New York: Viking, 1975.

The formula carries over into two subsequent collaborations with Jean Mohr: ***A Seventh Man: Migrant Workers In Europe*** (designed by Richard Hollis), published in 1975; and ***Another Way of Telling***, from 1982. Both continue to be built on the principle that, however interwoven, images and words should be approached on their own terms. Images rarely if ever simply illustrate the text writes Berger: "The photographs…say things which are beyond the reach of words. The pictures in sequence make a statement: a statement which is equal and comparable to, but different from, that of the text." Image and

Another Way of Telling / John Berger and Jean Mohr (with Nicolas Philibert) / New York: Pantheon Books, 1982.

text float free from the clutter of captions and attributions, rhythmically alternating between attention to particulars and commonplaces, between the private and public dimensions of the lives of ordinary individuals. Even if the interplay is loose, they work in concert.

Edmund Carpenter's brilliant media-anthropological explorations adopt a more disjunctive approach. A sensory anthropologist with wide experience in Canadian public radio and television, Carpenter belonged to the McLuhan

They Became What They Beheld
Edmund Carpenter /
Photographed by Ken
Heyman / Designed by
Hess and/or Antupit /
New York: Outerbridge
& Dienstfrey, Ballatine
Books, 1970.

inner circle. He cofounded the review *Explorations* and codirected the Ford Foundation seminar that led to the publication of *Explorations in Communication* (1960). In 1970, Carpenter published the first of three experimental books in a photo-essayistic vein: ***They Became What They Beheld*** (1970). The book was born as an essay on fashion as a language ghostwritten by Carpenter to cover for McLuhan (who was combatting the effects of a serious stroke). Published in *Harper's Bazaar*, it resurfaces in a typophotographic volume that opens with a sequence of three surreal photographs tagged as:

DISLOCATIONS. Only connect; the rest is silence.

Each image shows individuals in a familiar setting: a forest cemetery, an urban beachfront, the front porch of a row house. Their gazes, cast in a multitude of directions, appear radically disconnected. An explanation follows:

This notebook of juxtaposed images and explorations is organized around correspondences between certain preliterate & postliterate experiences. To convey the essence of these experiences to a contemporary audience, in the idiom of our day, I felt it necessary to find literary expressions consonant with the experiences themselves. The rhythms practiced here are heightened, concentrated & frequently more violent than those found in more conventional texts. They belong to the world of icon & music, graffiti & cartoon, and lie closer, I believe, to the original experiences.

The book's core theme is humanity's propensity to imitate its own creations. The Javanese dancer imitates the Javanese puppet; the '60s beauty mimes the look of a '60s television set or a lightbulb. But whereas the former inhabits a world of stable identities and identifications, the latter inhabits a world in which the I contains multitudes: "a world of electronic all-at-onceness in which everybody begins to include everybody else & many begin to feel the loss of their private identities." The result is fluid sense of self, marked by a closing photograph of a nature boy wearing a leaf mask, anticipated in the book's opening image of an eye peering through a cloth aperture.

Eskimo Realities
Edmund Carpenter /
Photographed by Eberhard
Otto, Fritz Spiess, and
Jørgen Meldgaard /
Designer: Arnold Skolnick /
New York: Holt, Rinehart
and Winston, Inc., 1973.

Carpenter followed his initial experiment with two additional volumes: *Oh, What a Blow That Phantom Gave Me!* (1972) and **Eskimo Realities** (1973). The first, perhaps his most famous, borrows its title from the lead volume of Cervantes's *Don Quixote*. It cross-cuts field notes and diary entries with theoretical analyses of media revolutions with a sampling of photographs. It concludes with a sharp critique of anthropology, wittily entitled "Misanthropology." The second book was designed by the creator of the Woodstock Music Festival poster, Arnold

Skolnick. It provides an eloquent, graphically spacious meditation on Eskimo culture and art in which white (and sometime black) voids enfold sparse scatterings of animated objects and drawings.

album • art

The paperback book that dreams of becoming a magazine doesn't always have a literary vocation. Sometimes that vocation is musical or cinematographic, sometimes both. Such was the case of several of the defining paperback experiments of the late 1960s. The territory they set out to explore is the potential crossover zone between sound, the moving image, and the printed page.

From midcentury onward, the medium of print begins to assume an increasing role as a support for music and film subcultures, whether in the form of album and liner notes with narrative and even phototypographical components, press books for the promotion of movies, books based on film scripts (now increasingly integrated, thanks to the work of "packagers" and "producers"), not to men-

*Rock and Other
Four Letter Words*
Written and designed by
J. Marks / Photographed
by Linda Eastman /
New York: Bantam
Books, 1968.

tion the long-standing tradition of film and novel adaptations and dialogues. But the alternative musical and film press, as well as fanzines, remained in an inchoate state of development until the 1970s.

Into the incubator strut publishing ventures like J. Marks's *Rock and Other Four Letter Words*: like its immediate model *The Medium Is the Massage*, at once an original paperback and an LP recording. With more than a bit of swagger, the book and record are dedicated to Karlheinz Stockhausen "who destroyed our ears so we could hear!" (Jack Marks, alias the pseudo-Cherokee intellectual "Jamake Highwater," was a gay Greek-American

J Marks, was born in Los Angeles in 1942, graduated from high school at 13, and had his Ph.D. at 20. Since then he has become a counter-culture legend, his movies have won awards, his photos have been shown at leading museums, his articles have starred in every underground magazine, his book and record album, ROCK AND OTHER FOUR LETTER WORDS, have been best sellers. J Marks is the pen name for Jamake Mamake Highwater.

dancer, writer, and self-mythologizer named Markropoulos who some have confused with the experimental filmmaker Gregory Markopoulos.)

Like many of Agel's INVENTORY BOOKS, the volume has no table of contents, no page numbers, no running headers or index. It is built instead like a sort of structured improvisation, alternately loose and tight, predictable and unpredictable, lively and even compelling in a rough cut-and-paste way. It begins with "ROCK IS!" pushing across a white page over a page from the dictionary (a quotation mosaic follows where rock is characterized as "ultimate," "American," "erotic," "real," "full of danger," "deranged," "unnatural," and "mystic"). It concludes with the same layout replayed as "ROCK IS!" (minus the dictionary page). In between these bookends is a succession

of bite-sized verbal-visual portraits, a kind of Facebook for some fifty-plus bands. Additional themes are spliced into the filmstrip at irregular intervals: an excursus on multichannel recording on the flip side of a foldout genealogical tree of pop music in the form of an integrated circuit board; an account of the lead performance venues and light shows; a twenty-page sequence in which a Rick Griffin poster morphs into *Saint John Beholding the Seven Golden Candlesticks* from Albrecht Dürer's *Apocalypse*; a four-page Grateful Dead foldout at "dead center" of the book; two pages on rock promoters; and a cutout page devoted to "Mr. Jones" in which the face of "Mr. Jones" is cut out from page **23** of *The Medium Is the*

Bob Dylan:
Don't Look Back
D. A. Pennebaker /
Designed by Carol Inouye /
New York: Ballantine
Books, 1968.

Massage. The typography is eclectic and the text a collage of quotations with the occasional bit of sermonizing: "Free-form rock, with its electronic overtones, is daringly close to the kind of concert music which the avant-garde failed for years to sell to the cultural elite. Kids discovered Stockhausen and Berio: the epitome of mature aesthetic achievement. The electronic composers seem as meaningless, violent and degenerate as the feed-back of the Jefferson Airplane."

A more sober and disciplined version of the same approach may be found in a number of film paperbacks from the period, such as the Ballantine companion to D. A. Pennebaker's ***Don't Look Back***. Here transcriptions of scenes and statements by the director, protagonist, and crew track alongside image sequences on various

scales from mini film strips to full sequences based on
page = frame equations. The book is designed to operate as a theater that invites viewers to play/replay the film
as if they were there in the editing room, overseeing the
final cut.

magazine • book

The same paperback revolution that transformed the publishing industry between the 1930s and the 1970s blurred the line of demarcation between magazines and books. In the new print communications landscape that resulted, books could be sold by subscription, drugstores and newsstands also became bookstores, and prestigious patrician publishing houses began to consort with once reviled pulp magazine factories. Magazine publishers started developing lines of books (*Time-Life*) and book publishers, lines of magazines (Grove). The business of publishing gradually converged with the movie, television, and music industries.

One significant but fragile consequence of this realignment was the emergence of the paperback literary magazine. The genre was forged by pioneers like:

— *The Penguin New Writing* digest, published 1940–50
— the New American Library's *New World Writing*, published 1952–59; and revived as *New American Review* between 1967 and 1977
— *Evergreen Review*, a quarterly published in the form of an octavo-sized trade paperback between 1957 and 1964

These ventures and others like them were developed along the lines of literary digests and almanacs. Unlike mainstream counterparts like *Reader's Digest*, they prided themselves on being elite "writers' magazines," with the ability to reach out to a "relatively mass audience" (the phrase is Theodore Solotaroff's from *New American Review*'s premiere issue). Though they often cross boundary lines *within* the realm of writing, they remained text-centered. The word *advertising* is willfully absent from their vocabulary.

Pressured by the rise of the alternative and rock press (*Rolling Stone*, *Crawdaddy*), the paperback literary magazine briefly veers off in a phototypographical direction around the time of the publication of *The Medium Is the Massage*. Some existing reviews like *Evergreen* alter their format from octavo to glossy quarto, anchoring every issue in erotic photographs. Others, like Ralph Ginzburg's *Avant-Garde* (1968–71), designed by Herb Lubalin, ride the

*US: A Paperback
Magazine 1*
Richard Goldstein
(editor in chief)
Sayre Ross (production)
John Gerbino (art director)
June 1969

*US: The Paperback
Magazine 2*
Richard Goldstein
(editor in chief)
Sayre Ross (production)
John Gerbino (art director)
October 1969

*US: The Paperback
Magazine 3*
Richard Goldstein
(editor in chief)
Sayre Ross (production)
Bill Skurski (art director)
May 1970

high (art) road toward luxury hardcover solutions not unlike those adopted by *Horizon* back in the 1950s.

US: A Paperback Magazine takes the opposite tack. Squarely (if momentarily) embedded in the space between the alternative press and mainstream media, it represents an experimental incursion on the part of Bantam Books into the youth market. Sold issue by issue (not by subscription), it mixes underground comics (Robert Crumb, Victor Moscoso, Spain, Peter Bramley), concrete (Richard Kostelanetz) and free verse poetry (Ed Sanders, Jim Morrison, Tom Clark, Ted Berrigan), and a hodgepodge of articles ranging from profiles of the Living Theater, Jack Kerouac, Timothy Leary, and Rex Reed, to personal/political pieces (Nikki Giovanni, Ellen Willis). The

tone is mischievous and the prose unfussy (with four-letter words welcome), but the overall editorial standards are solid. The review's graphic style remains eclectic, paced by visuals cast in a pop psychedelic mold, low-end photo collages, photocopied title pages, and a high degree of typographical variability. A few pieces are built around a cut-and-paste aesthetic, like Richard Meltzer's "TZ Glide" in issue 3: a pastiche of *TV Guide*. Others, like Editor in Chief Richard Goldstein's "Wrap" introduction to the inaugural issue, assume the form of a quotation mosaic à la Agel featuring the wisdom

of A. A. Milne, Marshall McLuhan, John Lennon, and Richard Nixon, as well as anonymous conversationalists. The theme is intergenerational: "A generation is a unit of experience...we are all our parents' saboteurs."

US survived only three issues before Bantam pulled the plug, unlike less commercial counterparts such as the Montreal-based **Mainmise**, the graphically lively counterculture monthly successfully published by Jean Basile, Georges Khal, et Christian Allègre between 1970 and

  1980. Accordingly, *US* never fully hit its graphic stride. But there are flashes of wit here and there. In issue 1, a press photograph of the teen serial killer Charles Starkweather appears first so close up that the oversized benday dots abstract away the face, then at middle distance, then at fully legible distance, at four-to-five-page intervals. In issue 2, a Duane Michals flip-book sequence appears in the upper right-hand corner, showing a long-haired youth performing a gun drill. (The legend atop the table of contents reads, "This is my rifle, this is my gun, one is for fighting, one is for fun.") Bill Skurski's pop collages alternate with commercial illustrations from a Special Forces Handbook in issue 3.

If the pop paperback magazine genre died with *US*, it soon returned in at least two guises: one pulp—*Destinies: The Paperback Magazine of Science Fiction and Speculative Fact* was founded in 1978; the other literary—*Granta* assumed the "paperback magazine" mantle when it was relaunched with support from Penguin in 1979. But the most fertile interpreter of these various legacies is V. Vale's now celebrated *RE/search*, the glossy paperback descendant of the legendary punk zine *Search and Destroy*.

The notion that the real, relayed through the artful interplay of "authentic" voices in the form of testimonials,
"authentic" images in the form of photographs, documents, and statistical data, can be made to speak in
a voice of protest has deep roots in modern media history. It informs a wide array of artifacts: from books like
Jacob Riis's *How the Other Half Lives: Studies among the
Tenements of New York* (1890) and New Deal descen-
dants like James Agee and Walker Evans's *Let Us Now
Praise Famous Men* (1941), to the documentary cinema to
political pamphlets and posters.

　　　The agitprop books of the late 1960s and early 1970s
run the above enterprise through the candy-colored tan-
gerine-flaked wringer of pop with highly variable outcomes.
At the sober end of the spectrum are black-and-white

*Right On!: A Documentary
on Student Protest*
Maryl Levine and John
Naisbitt / Designed by
David L. Burke / New York:
Bantam Books, 1970.

paperback originals like ***Right On!***, which packages a
1969 Urban Research Corporation study of protests on
292 university campuses as a documentary pamphlet-
album-book. The graphic concept developed by David L.
Burke, the Chicago-based designer called in by Bantam

on the project, remembered for his logo work, graphics for Teleflex, Burko lettering, and acrylic plastic designs, is simple and bold. In a volume built around racial politics, play black against white; limit the grays. In the absence of

Woodstock Nation: A Talk-Rock Album Abbie Hoffman, design by Concert Hall Publications, New York: Vintage, 1969.

a conventional apparatus, the structural core is provided by thirty numbered quotations concerning the debate over black studies, printed in white Linofilm Helvetica on black pages. Indexed at the back of the book, these are distributed at regular intervals from beginning to end and placed in dialogue with a cacophony of quotations and materials printed on white backdrops. As per Agel and Fiore's practice, the title page arrives belatedly (on p. 8) after four disjunctive double-page layouts. Phototypographic rhythms pace the narrative, regularly switching back and forth between billboardlike full-pages and smaller quotations, documents (letters, posters, photographs, photocopies) reproduced in varying degrees of resolution from full gray

scale to fully solarized, cartoons from the mainstream and alternative press, and multipage sequences (a banner, a march over a bridge, a protest rally). Burke's aim? "[O]n a severely limited budget, to capture the spirit of the conflict between the establishment and the students in a book form that can compete with other news media" (designarchives.aiga.org).

At the psychedelia/pop/politics/alt end of the spectrum comes Abbie Hoffman's **Woodstock Nation** "talk-rock

album" and its direct descendant, Gary Grimshaw's polychrome collection of White Panther Party leader John Sinclair's outlaw writings. The Hoffman book, designed by Concert Hall publications and

dedicated to Lenny Bruce, anthologizes the Yippie leader's thoughts in the festival's wake. It mixes a "foreplay" with ruminations on life and revolution, a (fake) handwritten "last letter of Che Guevara," an outline of *Yippie—The Movie*, and a "battle of the bands" fought out between the Who's "We're Not Gonna Take It" and a Yippie commentary. Cast in the mold of a counterculture rag, the album is animated by photos of the festival, political cartoons, Dover book dingbats, and collaged-in pages from an Army field manual. In the larger format Vintage edition, the chromatics oscillate unpredictably between white, black, red, blue, purple, and green. A mass-market scaled-down version was printed in sober black-and-white.

Grimshaw was the light show and poster designer for Detroit's Grande Ballroom, home to the MC5, and a leading figure in the campaign to free Sinclair (who in 1969 had been sentenced to ten years in prison for possession of marijuana). So, here, the graphic concept is not BW =

black versus white but rather, in the spirit of Woodstock Nation, a sequence of rainbow-colored signatures in a book dedicated to the Rainbow Nation and the Rainbow People's Party: a book that "talks about a lot of different things, but mostly it's a book about rock and roll music and the new life-form which has grown up around the music— the rainbow culture is what we call it" (p. **5**). The book's apparatus and typography are conventional with a table of contents, standard pagination, running headers, and two appendixes: one documenting the work of the party; the other in the form of a "Rainbow Reading & Listening List." Woven in between a chronologically organized sequence

Guitar Army: Street Writings/Prison Writings
John Sinclair / Designed by Jay Grimshaw / New York: Douglas Book Corporation, 1972.

of Sinclair's texts—alternative press writings, interviews, trial transcripts—is a visual apparatus mixing concert photos, psychedelic posters (including Grimshaw's own), press photographs of Sinclair and several White Panther political actions, and panels from radical comics. As if performing a light show on paper, color displaces typography as a framing device. There are pages with quotation mosaics. The overall effect is albumlike. **Guitar Army** is a counterculture fan rag dressed up like a mass-market paperback. An anthology for insiders, it is dedicated to all the electronic aborigines of the Rainbow Nation.

shelf • help

The breach in the realm of conventional paperback publishing opened up by the typophotographic experiments of the late 1960s gave rise not only to new forms of political and cultural argument addressed to mass audiences (unlike art publishing counterparts such as Something Else Press), but also to new expressions of the self ranging from the philosophical to the psychedelic-poetic.

The spectrum of such books of the self is broad. At the lyrical-philosophical end lies *Stuff, Etc.* (1970), a volume compiled by "John Gordon." Also assigned authorship of the script for the 1967 hit musical *You're a Good Man, Charlie Brown*, John Gordon was the nom de plume of the composer/songwriter/writer/actor Clark Gesner. In the course of a career of shuttling back and forth between the theater and children's television (*Captain Kangaroo*, *Mister Mayor*, The Children's Television Workshop), Gesner compiled what he called a "collection": a cut-and-paste assemblage of data, messages, flashes of information, guides, advertisements—the "steady stream of little voices, whis-

Stuff, Etc.
John Gordon /
New York: J. B.
Lippincott
Company, 1970.

pers, murmurs coming to us from everywhere else, talking to us, nudging us, getting us through from moment to moment." Gesner formulates his own counter-message and massage as a bulwark against the anesthetizing effects of this barrage by means of a handwritten first-person script that meanders in and out of the fractured

78-187880
Ira Einhorn / Designed and photographed by Marshall Henrichs / Garden City: Doubleday & Co., Inc., 1972.

debris of everyday life. Gesner's (mechanically repro-duced) handwriting here speaks in the voice of a restored interiority. It summons the reader to turn inward, away from the din: to listen to "the quietly unfolding set of per-sonalized instructions that has been ticking off steadily inside of each of us for all this time."

At the high end of the spectrum arrives Ira Einhorn's hallucinatory epic *78-187880*, with its Library-of-Congress-catalog-card-number-inspired title and design by Marshall Henrichs (who also crafted Maurice Stein and Larry Miller's inventive *Blueprint for Counter Education* [1970]). The book serves up a heady brew of lysergic reasoning in vintage philosophese (synergy, negentropy, noo-sphere), astrological symbols, physics talk (E=MC² to quarks), buckminsterfullerisms, vedic allusions, psycho-

analysis, and, most of all, environmental apocalypticism. Laid out as if a Poundian *Canto* crossbred with a Fuller poem on industrialization, the visual rhythms and textures echo Fiore and Agel. A pop surrealist look prevails. Close-ups of the human body abound, as do grainy clippings from newspapers, always printed full page. The poet, with

"a middle class Jewish past, a planetary present & a future that is cosmic [is] sitting writing here in Philadelphia" but contemplates "the continual rapid convergence toward the noosphere." His epic, pointed at planet Poesis, lands instead on planet Psycho. (Yes, our psychedelic poet is *the* Ira Einhorn: the radical environmentalist and "Unicorn killer" now serving a life sentence for the murder of Holly Maddux after twenty years on the run.)

As If—

Design
Producers

Afterword

Andrew Blauvelt

and Its

The fact that the designer **Quentin Fiore**'s name appears on the cover of ***The Medium Is the Massage***—and at the same size as, albeit below, the book's author **Marshall McLuhan**—signaled that the traditional hierarchies of the publishing world of 1967 were being turned if not upside down, then at least inside out. Typically destined to appear on the copyright page along with many other players (including **Jerome Agel**), such a design credit was and is an unusual practice. However, such a gesture looks both necessary and appropriate because what follows on the pages within is more a series of photomontages or collages than the dutiful typeset lines found in a typical paperback book. Similar cover recognition was given to designer **Bruce Mau**, in 1995, with the publication of ***S,M,L,XL***, a tome documenting the work and ideas of architect **Rem Koolhaas**. In both cases what was being acknowledged was the unusual circumstance of design's ability to transform the normative assumptions around what a book could be. This kind of double billing, under a sign of coauthorship, elevates the status of the designer and calls his role out among others—authors, translators, editors, printers, and publishers—in particular acts of publishing.

Questions about the designer's role in the publishing process have certainly preoccupied the design world for decades now. In fact, interest in projects like those by Fiore and McLuhan, where the lines or roles between different agents in the publishing process are crossed or blurred, seems to spike in moments when the designer's relationship to the book-making process is under revision or exploration.[1] Certainly, Fiore's layout approach was inspirational for many other books in the years immediately following its publication—from the late 1960s to the early 1970s. But a revived interest in this work took place in the early 1990s when two simultaneous phenomena were at play: one formal, the other technological.

The formal experimentation in page layout strategies that began in earnest in the 1980s was premised on the idea that reading itself had changed because of the impact of visual media on culture—television, film, advertising, music videos, and early computers. This thesis argued that readers were consuming smaller, more concise amounts of text (the sound bite), and were accustomed to more rapid juxtapositions of images and hybrid blends of media (music videos), all of which stood in stark contrast to the static literary conventions of the typical book page. As the design historian **Frances Butler** observed in 1989: "It may be that the incomplete story, the particle, the fragment, is now the preferred unit of information for our culture, and lack of place is more useful for presenting these fragments than to fix them into sentences or grids."[2] These explorations in form were made possible because by the mid-1980s the Macintosh computer had already begun to revolutionize the practice of graphic design. Suddenly, designers had much more control over the production of their work. The segmentation of labor involved in the printing process became more integrated as designers took on the work of typesetters, layout artists, and photomechanical technicians. With the advent of desktop publishing, the tasks of authorship (writing and editing) could be joined with those of production (typesetting and layout), fully integrating them into one machine and, potentially, in the hands of one person: the designer. Perhaps not surprisingly, this era spawned the concept of the designer as author, which did not necessarily mean designers writing books but rather trading on the cachet of the author as the originator of a work.[3] An assertion of authorship on the part of designers was a way to recast their perceived subordinate role in the production process by, for instance, taking their lead not from a client message brief but from the content at hand, initiating work on their own without the commission of a client, or working in a more entrepreneurial fashion. The more widespread interpretation of the concept, however, stressed freedom of personal expression for designers. As one of the primary texts on the subject put it: "These designers are interested in expression over style."[4]

By 1996 the designer and critic Michael Rock wrote the polemical essay "The Designer as Author," which sought to debunk this appropriation by designers as a way of laying claim to content creation or authorship.[5] Rooted in the rhetoric of poststructuralism, these claims were seen by Rock as ironic gestures, since theorists such as Roland Barthes and Michel Foucault had already pronounced the "death of the author" in the late 1960s.[6] Interestingly, Rock speculates on other possible metaphors for the designer's expanded role: designer as translator, designer as performer, or designer as director. Despite Rock's best attempts, none of these monikers stuck, and paradoxically his critique was misinterpreted by many as a call to arms for a new kind of graphic authorship in which the key to form making (design) was through the generation and control of content.

This focus on content represented a major shift in the design process—one that ultimately divided the modern from the postmodern. Typically content is preexisting, a given, provided by the client in a commissioning situation. In the modernist purview, good design does not depend on good content but on good form. However, it is also widely accepted that form derived from content is the graphic design equivalent of the modernist credo, form follows function. In the latter situation, it would appear that form depends on content for its expression. How do we reconcile these apparently divergent statements? An answer arrives when we consider form itself as its own kind of content. Such thinking is fully consistent with the conception of modern design as constituting its own language, a visual language, which is constructed and manipulated (controlled) by the designer. Rock also compares the graphic designer with the filmmaker—who often is not the scriptwriter, cinematographer, editor, or art director yet fashions from these disparate roles a coherent vision and may, if consistent in that quest, develop a recognizable body of work, a signature style: the designer as auteur. As Rock, evoking the preeminent modernist designer **Paul Rand**, succinctly puts it: "The content is, in short, always Design itself."[7]

From a postmodern perspective, however, form did not equal content. Content was independent from form, a source of inspiration as well as a constraint on textuality and meaning that could be used to guide design or as an inspirational point of departure. Content was also seen as intrinsically political, not simply a message but a statement. The injection of content, particularly new content, into the design process sought to yield new forms, and it did.[8] What it did not do, however, is sufficiently alter the systems and strictures in place for how design operates in the first place. In many ways, this concept of graphic authorship was a distraction from the fundamental changes being wrought on the practice of graphic design and its implications on the future of publishing. Many designers were quick to acknowledge and use the computer as a new tool—perhaps a kind of meta design tool—for formal experimentation and expedited processes, but were less likely to explore its potential as a machine that transformed the means of production while opening up new possibilities for distribution, the very promise of desktop publishing.

In retrospect, the advocates of design authorship might have been better served by the German critic Walter Benjamin's thesis, "The Author as Producer," written in 1934.[9] Argued within the changing communications environment of the early twentieth century (influenced by the popularization of radio, film, photography, and mass advertising) and informed by a Marxist philosophy that privileged the means of production, Benjamin sought to transform the role of the author in social-political terms. For him it was not simply enough for the writer to adopt political content without also transforming the systems of its production. Breaking down the barriers that bourgeois society had erected in production of texts was seen as a revolutionary act. More specifically, he takes up the use of photography in forms of mass media and "the barrier between words and pictures":

> What we should demand from photography is the capacity of giving a print a caption which would tear it away from fashionable clichés and give it revolutionary use-value. But we will pose this demand with the greatest insistence if we—writers—take up photography. Here too technical progress is the basis of political progress for the author as producer.[10]

Benjamin sought to rejoin production and consumption, imagining a better system, one "that is capable of making co-workers out of readers or spectators."[11] It is not a difficult leap to make from this historic proclamation to today's world of peer production, open platforms, and user-generated content. Indeed, the designer and writer Ellen Lupton puts forward a persuasive argument and yet another metaphor in her essay "The Designer as Producer," drawing on Benjamin's thesis. Lupton connects Benjamin's concept of production to the transformation of design's labor through a technological, rather than political, revolution, one that brings the designer in closer relation to the fabrication of his or her own work:

> The "desktop revolution" that began in the mid-1980s brought these [production] roles back into the process of design. The proletarianization of the editorial process offers designers a new crack at materialism, a chance to reengage the physical aspects of our work. Whereas the term "author," like "designer," suggests the cerebral workings of the mind, "production" privileges the activity of the body. Production is rooted in the material world. It values things over ideas, making over imagining, practice over theory.[12]

It's not only the materiality of design but also the notion of craft and technique that reemerges in the discourse once the designer has rejoined the production process. This change can be seen in the resurgent interest in older printing technologies, such as silkscreen and letterpress printing, or even the renewed interest in printed matter itself after years of design's virtualization (interface design, web design, motion graphics, and other screen-based forms). But many of these activities can be easily dismissed as nostalgic revivals of outdated technologies and processes or unbridled technological optimism. Either way, changing the method of production is not the same as transforming the means of production. As Lupton writes, "There exists opportunities to seize control—intellectually and economically—of the means of production, and to share that control with the reading public, empowering them to become producers as well as consumers of meaning."[13]

Today, more systematic experimentation is underway. Instead of role reversals and appropriating the tasks of others in the publishing process, designers have undertaken the exploration of publishing itself. The technological changes ushered in by the desktop publishing revolution have also been furthered by changes to the printing and distribution of books, such as document printers (machines capable of printing and binding entire books), and the advent of print-on-demand publishing services, where inventory is eliminated. These technological changes have been met by the continued conflation and expansion of roles in the publishing process by designers. The designer as publisher is but the latest variation in the decades-old struggle to emancipate design's productive labor.

Perhaps the most complete embodiment of the designer as publisher, Jop van Bennekom undertakes a variety of roles: creative director, art director, editor, and publisher. Trained as a graphic designer, van Bennekom collaborated with the journalist Gert Jonkers on *RE-*, *Butt*, *Fantastic Man*, and *The Gentlewoman*, which represent a fusion of editorial position and writing married to a unique design approach, whether the subject matter is gay male sexuality or men's or women's fashion. Other designers have also begun publishing ventures, notably Stuart Bailey and Peter Bil'ak who began the journal *Dot, Dot, Dot* in 2000. Forgoing the type of portfolio magazine that has come to dominate the design industry, *Dot, Dot, Dot* instead takes design as a point of departure in its wide-ranging subject matter. Unlike *Émigré* magazine in the

1990s—another example of the designer as publisher that championed the era's notion of designer as author—*Dot, Dot, Dot* opens a different discursive space for design, one that encourages a network of designers to write not only about design but also about other subjects. It is perhaps most influential on a younger generation of designers as a publishing experiment in and of itself, instructive in its eclectic subject matter and its typographic layout, and also for its production and printing choices.

Winterhouse is a design studio, a print publisher of literature, and an online publisher of the various aggregated websites under the **DesignObserver.com** banner. Winterhouse published ***The National Security Strategy of the United States of America*** in 2002. Its text was the official policy report issued by the administration of **President George W. Bush**, outlining a dramatic shift in American foreign policy—the codification of the Bush doctrine. By reprinting and circulating this document in a wider space, freeing it from governmental archives and media interpretations of its content, Winterhouse sought to stimulate public discourse on the subject. This subtle but radical gesture attempted to reconnect with traditional ideals of a free press as a vital agent in civic democracy. The project calls to mind **A. J. Liebling**'s famous statement: "Freedom of the press is guaranteed only to those who own one."[14]

Ultimately, access to the means of production and distribution has been most democratized, as desktop publishing was joined to digital book printing and online distribution. The advent of self-publishing through print-on-demand services such as Lulu.com has marked an important moment in the history of publishing. Although the concept of the vanity press has been around since the birth of publishing, the rise of Internet-enabled self-publishing has opened the doors to a much larger pool of potential authors, who, because of circumstance more than choice, act as their own editor, designer, and promoter. Perhaps not surprisingly, professional publishing companies cast a skeptical eye toward the possibilities of any real crossover success in mainstream publishing terms (i.e., the best-seller hit) for most of these authors. The most prolific self-publisher is **Philip M. Parker**, a business professor, who has produced more than one hundred thousand books using a fully automated process to conduct online research, writing, and layout to publish printed books and to issue digital reports on a mind-boggling range of topics, from a time line of anime to medical sourcebooks on restless leg syndrome or sales forecast reports for lemon-flavored bottled water in Japan. Parker's "long-tail" approach—selling small volumes of unique items to many niche customers—and the near elimination of human labor have produced an inverted publishing venture, one where a detailed report highly beneficial to just a few or even one person can yield a profit, with prices ranging from about $25 to nearly $800.

Designers have also begun using print-on-demand services as a convenient method of self-publishing their own work, albeit within the tight design parameters (restricted page size, paper stock, and cover materials, etc.) imposed on the process from these services. Issues of binding accuracy and print quality have also hampered the extent to which designers would be interested in using this particular process. ***Dear Lulu*** is a self-published "calibration book" created during a residency of the designer **James Goggin** with faculty and students at the Hochschule Darmstadt, in Germany in 2008. Its ninety-six pages contain a variety of colors, patterns, lines, textures, photographs, and typography in order to test the quality of Lulu.com. This practical demonstration project merges the kind of technical knowledge that one might find in conventional design production classes with a Web 2.0 approach to collaborative learning—an act of pedagogical publishing.

Partly as a reaction to the design limits of print-on-demand publishing, some designers are resorting to purchasing their own digital printing equipment, a circumstance that allows them to control the process to a greater extent. **Urs Lehni**, a Swiss graphic designer, established **Rollo Press** in 2008. Working with an old Risograph GR 3770 machine, a digital duplicating machine that is faster and cheaper than laser printers or photocopiers, Rollo seeks to integrate all steps of the publishing process: "from concept to design on to printing, binding and distribution."[15] A limited palette of black and a handful of ink colors underscore an aesthetic philosophy that deliberately rejects the ubiquitous availability of and desire for full-color printing. **Birch**, a London-based design studio, has started **Black Box Press**, also armed with a Riso duplicator, which offers "a not for profit platform for designers, writers and artists to publish their work and further collaborative projects."[16]

In 2006 Stuart Bailey and **David Reinfurt**, under the name **Dexter Sinister**, published a manifesto of sorts on its home page. In it they compared the production economies of the automobile world—the assembly-line method of Ford to the just-in-time model of Toyota—with that of the publishing world. Underscoring the flexibility of both the production process and the roles involved in it, they write:

> The prevailing model of professional practice is firmly entrenched in the Fordist Assembly-Line. Writing, design, production, printing, and distribution are each handled discretely by specialists as the project proceeds through a chain of command and production. Recently, laser printers, photocopiers, page-layout softwares, cellphones, and word processors have split this model wide open. A project might reasonably be written by the publisher who begins a layout and works with the designer who commissions a writer, and sources a printer that will produce fifty copies by Wednesday.[17]

A self-described "just-in-time workshop and occa-sional bookstore," Dexter Sinister as both a practice and a storefront conflates the sites of production and consump-tion. Will Holder, who collaborates with Bailey under the moniker Will Stuart, not only serves multiple roles, such as editor and designer of the journal *F.R. David*, but also explores publishing as a performative act. For instance, the second issue of the Will Stuart–produced journal, *Tourette's*, was realized as a weeklong festival of screen-ings, performances, talks, and concerts at the W139, an exhibition space in Amsterdam, instead of a printed vol-ume. Holder's interests in repetition, translation, and adap-tation speak to other aspects of the publishing process (e.g., reprints and revised editions) as much as the gen-eral concept of reworking. In 2008 Holder rewrote William Morris's 1890 utopian text, *News from Nowhere*, as *Middle of Nowhere*, a speculation about the coming century.

Fittingly, it was Morris's Kelmscott Press that cre-ated the private press movement in the last century, a reaction to the mass production of books that looked back to the fifteenth century for inspiration. As technologies for publishing move forward and continue to be decentral-ized, the attitude by some designers reaches backward, to a premodern conception of publishing. The particular roles and agents in the publishing process seem much less important than exploring the act itself—as if in one last act of appropriation: the designer as publisher. The following statement, attributed to Morris, can be found on the Rollo Press website: "To own the means of production is the only way to gain back pleasure in work, and this, in return, is considered as a prerequisite for the produc-tion of (applied) art and beauty."[18] Whether Morris spoke or wrote these words, the sentiment supports the con-temporary idea that design's destiny—indeed a designer's happiness—is tied to the most unfettered and direct acts of making.

Notes

Introduction:
The Cinematic Art of
Paperback Books

1. Eliot Fremont-Smith, "The Tedium Is the Message," Books of The Times, *New York Times*, September 4, 1968.

2. Quentin Fiore, "The Future of the Book," *Media and Methods*, December 1968, 20–26.

3. Quoted in *The Future of Time*, ed. Henri Yaker, Humphry Osmond, and Frances Cheek (Garden City, New York: Doubleday, 1971).

An Inventory of Inventories

1. Chuck Pulin, "Inside 2001—Interview with Jerome Agel," *Crawdaddy* 4.14 (1970): sect. 2, n.p.

2. Anonymous, "Paper Back Talk," *New York Times,* February 29, 1976.

3. László Moholy-Nagy, *Painting Photography Film*, trans. Janet Seligman (1925; repr. Cambridge, MA: MIT Press, 1973), 39.

4. Jan Tshichold, *The New Typography: A Handbook for Modern Designers*, trans. Ruari McLean (1928; repr. Berkeley: University of California Press, 1998), 92.

5. Le Corbusier, *Toward an Architecture*, trans. John Goodman, Texts and Documents (Los Angeles: Getty Research Institute, 2007), 42. The pamphlet itself is reproduced on page 2.

6. It is perhaps worth noting that the cover image recurs on page 154 but is mislabeled as "The Acquitania, Cunard Line," even though the Empress of Asia reappears once again only three pages later.

7. Walker Evans, "Foreword: James Agee in 1936," in James Agee and Walker Evans, *Let Us Now Praise Famous Men* (Boston: Houghton Mifflin, 1941), xv.

8. Erskine Caldwell and Margaret Bourke-White, *You Have Seen Their Faces* (New York: Modern Age Books, 1937), front leaf.

9. On Chicago Dynamic Week, see Daniel Bluestone, "Preservation and Renewal in Post–World War II Chicago," *Journal of Architectural Education* 47.4 (1994): 212–14. Agel would recall the event on the front page of the August 1967 issue of *Books*.

10. Eileen Lottman, "Under Covers," *Village Voice*, December 6, 1973.

11. Quoted in Peter Bart, "Advertising: Book Promotion is Defended," *New York Times,* October 25, 1962.

12. The incident is reported as "Boot-Jacket Model Discards Top in City," *New York Times,* February 7, 1969.

13. For a comprehensive account of this period, see Frank L. Schick, *Two-Bit Culture: The Paperbacking of America* (Boston: Houghton Mifflin, 1984). The websites paperbarn .www1.50megs.com/Paperbacks/ and www.crcstudio.org/paperbacks/ index.php contain some useful materials on the paperback revolution.

14. E. S. Carpenter, ed., *Explorations: Studies in Culture and Communication 2* (Toronto: University of Toronto Press, 1954), 11. The passage is mentioned in Sam Neill's comprehensive "Books and Marshall McLuhan," *Library Quarterly* 41 (October 1971): 316.

15. Marshall McLuhan, *Understanding Media: The Extensions of Man*, 2nd ed. (New York: Signet, 1966), 283–84.

16. The story of the review's foundation was recounted in "That's Show Biz," *Newsweek,* October 17, 1966, 103.

17. Display ad, *New York Times,* December 25, 1966.

18. "The Cocktail Party" proved so successful that, even after *Books* ceased publication in late 1968, Agel continued the column in Paul Krassner's *Realist*, where it appeared in the December 1968 and April 1969 issues. A successor column titled "Book Buzz" appeared in the *Washington Post* and *Times Herald* on January 18 and April 12, 1970.

19. The quote is from John Simon, interviewed by Agel, "A Reader's Guide to the John Simons," *Books,* May 1967, 3.

20. In Marvin Kitman's satirical review of the book, "Get the Message?" published on March 26, 1967, in the *New York Times*, Agel described himself as "the first co-ordinator in publishing history, which means I played the David Merrick, bringing together the sound and the music."

21. The episode is richly narrated in Tom Wolfe's essay "What If He Is Right?" later reprinted in *The Pump House Gang* (New York: Farrar, Straus and Giroux, 1968), 135–70. The essay's first iteration was "The New Life Out There," published in the *New York Herald Tribune,* November 21, 1965. In *The Virtual Marshall McLuhan* (Montreal: McGill University Press, 2001), 81–94, Donald Theall has provided a fine account of the packaging of McLuhan as a celebrity.

22. All three books were reissued in the wake of *The Medium Is the Massage*'s mass success: *The Mechanical Bride: Folklore of Industrial Man* was reissued by Beacon Press (Boston) in 1967; *Counterblast* was substantially reworked by Harley Parker for the 1969 Harcourt, Brace, and World (New York) edition; and *Verbi-Voco-Visual Explorations*, originally volume 8 of the journal *Explorations*, was reprinted by Something Else Press (New York) in 1967. Richard Schickel notes that McLuhan had written Frank Kermode "that the ideal form for the book would be an ideogram or perhaps a film, for he can think of no other way to create 'an inconclusive image that is lineal and sequential'" ("Marshall McLuhan: Canada's Intellectual Comet," *Harper's Magazine* 231, November 1965, 62–68). On this topic, see Donald Theall, "The Essai Concrète," in *The Medium Is the Rear View Mirror: Understanding McLuhan* (Montreal: McGill-Queen's University Press, 1971), 151–65.

23. Marshall McLuhan, *The Gutenberg Galaxy: The Making of Typographic Man* (New York: Signet Books, 1969), 7.

24. Agel to McLuhan, June 4, 1965, McLuhan Archive, National Library of

Canada, MG 31—D 156—Vol. 18—folder 10, hereafter cited as MA, folder 10.

25. The idea was taken up by Eric McLuhan at some later point and eventually became a volume edited by Marshall McLuhan, Kathy Hutchon, and Eric McLuhan, *City as Classroom: Understanding Language and Media* (Agincourt, Ont.: Book Society of Canada, 1977).

26. Quoted from an unpublished interview with Steven Heller and J. Abbott Miller dating from 1988. According to Fiore, a conversation about *Understanding Media* prompted him "to ask Agel, a publicist, 'packager' and publisher of *Books*, a monthly newspaper dealing with publishing matters, who had previously done some PR work for me, to suggest to Marshall McLuhan if he would be interested in working together on a picture/text book based on some of his thoughts." Elsewhere in the interview, however, Fiore is more ambiguous, implying that Agel thought of Fiore in relation to the project, not the other way around.

27. Agel to McLuhan, September 14, 1965, MA, folder 10; my emphasis.

28. Agel to McLuhan, December 16, 1965, MA, folder 10. A letter dated January 8, 1966, repeats the point: "Your role, as we have often discussed, would be of advisor and approver"; my emphasis.

29. Agel to McLuhan, February 19, 1966, MA, folder 10.

30. On page 203 of *The Medium and the Messenger* (Cambridge: MIT Press, 1989), Philippe Marchand notes that "seventeen publishers turned

down the proposal before Bantam Books agreed to take on the project."

31. Fuller to Agel, January 15, 1966, property of Nina Agel. The letter goes on to mention documentary film rights, which had evidently been part of Agel's January 8 proposal.

32. In a letter to McLuhan dated May 20, 1966, Agel wrote, "One last question, from the publishers: Is the title, 'The Medium Is the Massage: An Inventory of Effects,' your final choice? Fiore and I go for it, they go for it mildly, but there will be no objection if this is your final decision" (McLuhan Archive, National Library of Canada, MG 31—D 156—vol. 97—folder 37).

33. Jerome Agel, "A Reader's Guide to the John Simons," *Books,* May 1967, 3.

34. The "CBS-Columbia Records project" is first mentioned in a March 22, 1967, letter from Agel to McLuhan (MA, folder 10). The script was developed by Agel over the subsequent month. The recording session apparently took place in May, and editing was completed by June 12, with production underway immediately thereafter. Agel planned a three-hour boat cruise to promote the album's release.

35. Agel to McLuhan, April 28, 1967, MA, folder 10. The recording is available at www.ubu.com/sound/mcluhan.html.

36. "This Time the Medium Is the Mini," *New York Times,* July 20, 1967.

37. marshallmcluhan.com/faqs.html. The story was confirmed to me in an email message from Eric McLuhan,

dated August 29, 2010: "I was present during the entire time and can vouch for a typo as the source. It tickled Dad no end because it meant the title now had four levels of meaning, all relevant: the medium is the message, and the mess-age, and the massage, and the mass-age." There is yet another account that should be mentioned, put forth in Edmund Snow Carpenter's "That Not-So-Silent Sea," in Donald Theall, *The Virtual Marshall McLuhan* (Montreal: McGill-Queen's University Press, 2001), 236–61. According to Carpenter, the switch is attributable to Sam Zacks who, hearing an explanation of the phrase "the medium is the message," replied, "'You mean, like a massage?' At which point, message became massage, mass-age, mess-age, etc. etc."

38. W. Terrence Gordon, *Marshall McLuhan: Escape into Understanding: A Biography* (New York: Basic Books 1997), 175.

39. Marchand, *Medium and the Messenger*, 194.

40. The phrase is Neil Compton's, from "A Pot of Message," *Nation,* May 15, 1967, 631.

41. Eliot Fremont-Smith, "'All the World's a Sage,'" Books of The Times, *New York Times,* February 27, 1967. The phrase "McLuhan made easy" is from Marchand, *Medium and the Messenger*, 203.

42. Among the University of Michigan Press books were Marianne Thalmann, *The Romantic Fairy Tale: Seeds of Surrealism*, trans. Mary B. Corcoran (Ann Arbor: University of Michigan Press, 1964); Angelica Balabanoff, *Impressions of Lenin,*

trans. Isotta Cesari (Ann Arbor: University of Michigan Press, 1964); Leon Trotsky, *The New Course and the Struggle for the New Course*, trans. Max Shachtman (Ann Arbor: University of Michigan Press, 1965). The connection to *Crawdaddy* came about thanks to Agel, who had asked Paul Williams to write a piece for *Books* about his one-year-old review. Williams's essay appeared in the February 1967 issue of *Books* and Fiore's *Crawdaddy* cover appeared in the March 1967 issue of the review. Interestingly enough, both employ the convention of a photo sequence of headshots.

43. "Paper," *Industrial Design,* November 1958, 1–18. The essay was reprinted soon thereafter by the Tamarind Lithography Workshop in Los Angeles.

44. Among the editions Fiore produced for Franklin were Robert Fitzgerald's translations of the *The Iliad* and *The Odyssey* (1976), Euripides (1976), and Richard Burton's translation of *Tales from the Arabian Nights* (1977).

45. From a letter to William Jovanovich, in *Letters of Marshall McLuhan*, ed. Matie Molinaro, Corinne McLuhan, and William Toye (New York: Oxford University Press, 1987), 339.

46. The September 14, 1965 letter from Agel spoke of "an illustrated book based on your published works," with McLuhan acting as "adviser and approver" (*Letters of Marshall McLuhan,* 339–40).

47. "The book had in fact been composed by Jerome Agel, who had written a profile of McLuhan in

1965, and Quentin Fiore, a first-class book designer. The two selected or commissioned photographs to accompany excerpts they culled and reshaped from various writings and statements of McLuhan's.... McLuhan contributed the punning title and approved the text and layouts. Agel and Fiore evidently did their work well: McLuhan changed only one word. Their mix of text and visuals was indeed a virtuoso feat. They used arresting photographs and artwork and performed interesting experiments with type, laying it upside down, on the slant, or in mirror image, switching its size from page to page, switching between regular and boldface, and so on. Agel referred to the result as a 'cubist' production. McLuhan recognized that it was an effective sales brochure for his ideas" (Marchand, *Medium and the Messenger*, 192).

48. Agel to McLuhan, May 20, 1966, MA, folder 37. Evidently, the book changed considerably between the time of the letter and the final version. In his unpublished 1988 interview with Heller and Miller, Fiore notes that "we had conversations generally describing the book, but Marshall...was getting to the peak of his popularity. There were very, very great demands on his time. He was not available for discussions or interviews."

49. Perhaps the single closest match between a fully McLuhan authored text and *The Medium Is the Massage* is the talk typescript of his May 7, 1966, lecture at the Kaufmann Art Gallery, which bears the same title as the book. Its text has been reprinted in Marshall McLuhan, *Understanding Me: Lectures and Interviews*, ed.

Stephanie McLuhan and David Staines (Toronto: McLelland and Stewart, 2003), 76–97. Given the dating of this text, it is hard to establish whether the Fiore/Agel-developed typescript was already in existence.

50. Unpublished 1988 interview with Heller and Miller.

51. McLuhan, *Understanding Media*, 302.

52. The issue was accompanied by two illustrations from the microfilm edition, one reproduced on the cover and the other on page 167.

53. Marshall McLuhan, *Vision in Motion* (Chicago: Paul Theobald, 1947), 204. The student photograph is by O. George Morris Jr. In the 1988 interview with Heller and Miller, Fiore asserts that he was unfamiliar with *Verbi-Voco-Visual Explorations* at the time of *The Medium Is the Massage,* but the reworking of the Morris photograph suggests otherwise.

54. Unpublished 1988 interview with Heller and Miller.

55. Anthony Hodgkinson, "The Medium Is the Medium," *A V Communication Review* 15.3 (1967): 313. As the author notes, the hardcover edition reveals its status as a secondary by-product of the paperback original owing to its glued folios and deeper gutter.

56. Unpublished 1988 interview with Heller and Miller.

57. McLuhan, *Understanding Media*, 139.

58. In Marvin Kitman's humorous and, at times, parodic review, he singles out this image for criticism: "Many viewer-readers will also be puzzled by the art work, which is as hard to understand as anything McLuhan has written in the past. For example, what is the meaning of the picture on page 17?" ("Get the Message?," *New York Times*, March 26, 1967). Since Kitman knew Agel personally, was he in on the joke?

59. Quoted in Kitman, "Get the Message?"

60. Unpublished 1988 interview with Heller and Miller.

61. Jerome Agel, quoted in Kitman, "Get the Message?"

62. The identification was confirmed to me by Nina Agel. The page has so far resisted my efforts to fully decode it.

63. Unpublished 1988 interview with Heller and Miller.

64. "The Cocktail Party," *Books*, September 1966.

65. Kitman "Get the Message?"

66. Eliot Fremont-Smith, "'All the World's a Sage,'" Books of The Times, *New York Times*, February 27, 1967.

67. *Time*, March 3, 1967, 102.

68. Clarence Petersen, "Understanding McLuhan," *Chicago Tribune*, March 5, 1967.

69. Arthur Schlesinger Jr., *Book Week*, March 19, 1967.

70. Edmund Fuller, "Marshall McLuhan Keeps Plunging Ahead," *Wall Street Journal*, March 31, 1967.

71. Compton, "Pot of Message," 632.

72. Tom Nairn, *New Statesman*, September 22, 1967, 362.

73. Hodgkinson, "Medium Is the Medium," 313.

74. Unpublished 1988 interview with Heller and Miller.

75. *Aspen* 4 (Spring 1967).

76. Agel to McLuhan, November 23, 1966, MA, folder 10.

77. "As I indicated this morning, in working on the second book Quentin and I have been developing material on the general subject of education, where it is, where it could go. Bantam is prepared to pay now for a book on education that it paid for the upcoming automation book" (Agel to McLuhan, March 22, 1967, MA, folder 10). Discussion of this prospective venture continues on beyond the publication of *War and Peace in the Global Village*.

78. Email to the author, October 11, 2009.

79. McLuhan to Philip and Molly Deane, December 15, 1967, *Letters of Marshall McLuhan*, 348.

80. McLuhan to Humphrey, December 1, 1967, *Letters of Marshall McLuhan*, 349–50.

81. The genesis of this feature of *War and Peace in the Global Village* is discussed in Eric McLuhan, *The*

Role of Thunder in Finnegans Wake (Toronto: University of Toronto Press, 1997), xii–xiii. The book itself originated as a thesis written by Eric during this very period.

82. McLuhan, *Role of Thunder in Finnegans Wake*, xiv.

83. Unpublished 1988 interview with Heller and Miller.

84. Fiore to McLuhan, August 14, 1967, McLuhan Archive, National Library of Canada, MG 31—D 156—vol. 23—folder 76.

85. There are hints that Desmond Morris's much celebrated *The Naked Ape: A Zoologist's Study of the Human Animal* (London: Cape, 1967), mentioned on p. 161 of *War and Peace in the Global Village*, may have served as a model.

86. Tom Wolfe, "McLuhan: Through Electric Circuitry to God," *Chicago Tribune,* September 15, 1968.

87. Edmund Fuller, "Towards Understanding McLuhan's Message," *Wall Street Journal,* October 15, 1968.

88. Paul D. Zimmerman, "Massaging McLuhan," *Newsweek,* September 23, 1968, 102.

89. Eliot Fremont-Smith, "The Tedium Is the Message," *New York Times,* September 4, 1968.

90. "Fashion: A Bore War?" *Saturday Evening Post,* July 27, 1968, 29.

91. "We're also starting a new newspaper, 25,000 copies a week, available free…. It's called *Keep*

in Touch available free, weekly at Bookmasters nine stores" (Pulin, "Inside 2001").

92. Elias Canetti, "Touch," *Books,* June 1968, 5.

93. Fuller to Agel, January 15, 1966, property of Nina Agel.

94. Aison was hired by Agel and worked under his supervision. She was succeeded by Renich after four months because she was pregnant at the time. During the four months of her layout work on the book, Aison was unaware of Fiore ever having been directly consulted on layout decisions. When she inquired about asking for Fiore's approval for her mechanicals, she was told that this was unnecessary (telephone interview with the author, October 13, 2010). The story is confirmed by Fiore in his interview with Heller and Miller: "At that time I had to give out much of the work and mechanical preparation."

95. Telephone interview with the author, October 13, 2010.

96. "The Phantom Captain," *Nine Chains to the Moon* (Philadelphia: Lippincott, 1938), 18–19.

97. Pulin, "Inside 2001."

98. Ibid.

99. "What I Am Trying to Do," *Saturday Review,* March 2, 1968, 13. The text underwent a great many iterations. The version printed in *I Seem to Be a Verb* omits the first twenty-five words.

100. Pulin, "Inside 2001."

101. Unpublished 1988 interview with Heller and Miller.

102. In a recent interview with Jonah Raskin, Retherford stated: "I was the ghost writer for the book. That meant that I conceptualized the whole book and created a myth so that it would all hang together. I designed it so that it would look and feel like the six-o'clock news, and so it broke out of the linear mode. I was inspired by Quentin Fiore who had worked with Marshall McLuhan on *The Medium Is the Massage*; later we brought in Fiore to be the official designer, and I worked closely with him. That was a fabulous experience, and I went on to become a graphic designer." Quoted from http://theragblog.blogspot .com/2010/01/jonah-raskin-yippie- jerry-rubins-do-it.html.

103. Vincent Canby, "Spaced Out by Stanley," *New York Times,* May 3, 1970.

104. Carol Geduld, "Deeper in *Space Odyssey,*" *Literature/Film Quarterly* 2.2 (1974): 193.

105. The psychology books are the Radical Therapist Collective, *The Radical Therapist*, produced by Jerome Agel (New York: Ballantine Books, 1971); The Rough Times staff, *Rough Times*, produced by Jerome Agel (New York: Ballantine Books, 1973); and Humphry Osmond with John A. Osmundsen and Jerome Agel, *Understanding Understanding* (New York: Harper and Row, 1974). The conterfactual history book is *A World without...What Our Presidents Didn't Know (*New York: Toltec, 1972). The self-help books were Jo Ann York with Jerome Agel and Eugene Boe, *How I Feed My Family on $16 a Week*

(and Have Meat, Fish, or Poultry on the Table Every Night) (New York: Coward, McCann and Geoghegan, 1975); Allan Cott with Jerome Agel and Eugene Boe, *Fasting: The Ultimate Diet* (Toronto: Bantam Books, 1975) and *Fasting as a Way of Life* (Bantam: New York, 1977).

106. J. Abbot Miller, "Quentin Fiore: Massaging the Message," *Eye: The International Review of Graphic Design* 2.8 (1993): 46–55.

107. Ibid.

108. I am echoing the opening of *I Seem to Be a Verb*: "I live on Earth at present, and I don't know what I am. I know that I am not a category. I am not a thing—a noun. I seem to be a verb, an evolutionary process—an integral function of the universe" (R. Buckminster Fuller, with Jerome Agel and Quentin Fiore, *I Seem to Be a Verb* [New York: Bantam Books, 1970], 1).

109. Agel to McLuhan, February 2, 1973, McLuhan Archive, National Library of Canada, MG 31—D 156—vol. 18—folder 11.

110. Agel to McLuhan, April 9, 1973, MA, folder 11.

111. McLuhan to Agel, June 15, 1973, MA, folder 11.

112. Agel to McLuhan, March 20, 1978, MA, folder 11. Agel would go on to produce a book with this very title in collaboration with Osmond in 1981.

113. Agel to McLuhan, March 22, [1973?], MA, folder 11.

114. McLuhan to Agel, May 2, 1973, MA, folder 11.

115. Quentin Fiore, "The Future of the Book," in Henri Yaker, Humphry Osmond, and Frances Cheek, *The Future of Time, Man's Temporal Environment* (Garden City, NY: Doubleday, 1971).

116. Quoted in Fiore, "Future of the Book," 497.

Afterword:
As If: Design and Its Producers

1. Ellen Lupton and J. Abbott Miller were among the first to resurface the work of Quentin Fiore for Marshall McLuhan in 1993 (*Eye*, volume 2, number 8), subsequently reprinted in a book of their collected writings, *Design Writing Research* (New York: Princeton Architectural Press, 1996), 90-101.

2. Frances Butler, "Reading Outside the Grid: Designers and Society," reprinted in *Looking Closer: Critical Writings on Graphic Design* (New York: Allworth, 1994), 95. Butler cites McLuhan's aphoristic writing style (and by extension Fiore's and Agel's treatment) as a progenitor of this phenomenon. Butler's essay was originally published in *ACD Statements*, volume 4, number 3, Spring 1989.

3. Anne Burdick explores the intersections of design and writing in two issues of *Émigré* magazine (number 35, Summer 1995, and number 36, Fall 1995). Steven McCarthy and Cristina de Almeida hosted the conference and exhibition, *Designer as Author: Voices and Visions* at Northern Kentucky University in 1996, framing the discussion in terms of "self-authored design."

4. Katherine McCoy and David Frej, "Typography as Discourse," *I.D. Magazine*, March–April 1988, 34–37.

5. Michael Rock, "The Designer as Author," *Eye* 5.20 (1996): 44–53.

6. The "death of the author" occasioned the "birth of the reader," which formed the theoretical basis of why designers, who act as a bridge between authored messages from clients and the reader or audience, might be interested in multiple voices, alternative readings, and reevaluating design conventions that had been formed in more authored-centered periods. For a review of the use of this theory, see Ellen Lupton and J. Abbott Miller, "Deconstruction and Graphic Design," reprinted in *Design, Writing, Research*, 2–23.

7. Rock revisits "The Designer as Author," in his essay "Fuck Content" (2005), www.2x4.org/.

8. For a survey of the kinds of new work being produced, see Rick Poynor's trilogy of books: *Typography Now: The Next Wave* (London: Booth-Clibborn Editions, 1991), *The Graphic Edge* (London: Booth-Clibborn Editions, 1993), and *Typography Now II: Implosion* (London: Booth-Clibborn Editions, 1996).

9. Walter Benjamin, "The Author as Producer," trans. John Heckman, reprinted in *New Left Review*, July–August 1970.

10. Ibid.

11. Ibid.

12. Ellen Lupton, "The Designer as Producer," Steven Heller, ed., *The Education of a Graphic Designer*, 2nd ed. (New York: Allworth, 2005), 214–19.

13. Ibid., 161.

14. Abbott Joseph Liebling, "Do You Belong in Journalism?" *New Yorker*, May 4, 1960, 109.

15. "About," Rollo Press, accessed February 14, 2011, www.rollo-press .com/about/.

16. "About," Black Box Press, accessed February 14, 2011, www .blackboxpress.co.uk/about.php.

17. www.dextersinister.org/index .html?id=35. Posted online August 15, 2006.

18. This statement does not appear in the William Morris essay, "Art and Its Producers," as stated by Rollo, although its basic thrust is plausible. See www.rollo-press.com /about/. According to the William Morris Society, Morris made similar statements in other lectures, including this one from "Art and Socialism," delivered before the Secular Society of Leicester on January 23, 1884: "Nothing should be made by man's labour which is not worth making, or which must be made by labour degrading to the makers."

Image Credits

We kindly acknowledge permission
to include original cover and page
designs by Jerome Agel and Quentin
Fiore, courtesy of Gingko Press:
*The Medium Is the Massage: An
Inventory of Effects*; *War and Peace
in the Global Village*; *I Seem to Be a
Verb*; *The Making of Kubrick's 2001*;
*Is Today Tomorrow? A Synergistic
Collage of Alternative Futures*; *Herman
Kahnsciousness*; *Other Worlds*; and
It's About Time & It's About Time.
FCIT (Francis Rolt-Wheeler, *The
Boy with the U.S. Inventors* [Boston:
Lothrop, Lee & Shepard Co., 1920,
213]): 32. NASA: 172–73. Photos
by Peter Moore © Estate of Peter
Moore/VAGA, New York, NY: 58–63.
Random House: 197, 201, 206–7, 209,
210–11; illustration(s) copyright ©
1972 by Ira Einhorn, and jacket cover
copyright © 1972 by Anchor Books,
a division of Random House, Inc.,
from *78-187880* by Ira Einhorn,
design by Marshall Heinrichs. Used
by permission of Anchor Books,
a division of Random House, Inc.:
214–15.

Acknowledgments

Jeffrey T. Schnapp
The present essay would not have been possible without the generous assistance provided by Nina Agel, Walter Glanze, and Nick Falletta, who were willing to meet with me and to speak at length about Jerome Agel's life and career. I am particularly grateful to Nina for sparing me a great many factual errors. J. Abbott Miller was kind enough to dig up and share the transcripts of his and Steven Heller's 1988 interview with Quentin Fiore. Eric McLuhan patiently replied to a long stream of emails and offered too many clarifications and corrections to count. Cathryn S. Aison kindly shared her recollections of the production of *I Seem to Be a Verb* over the telephone. Graham Larkin has been unstinting in his support for this project and made a number of valuable suggestions that I incorporated into the text. A special thanks goes out to the three research assistants who brilliantly assisted me on this project: Giorgio Alberti (Stanford), Stephanie Frampton (Harvard), and Adam Welch (Toronto).

Adam Michaels
For wide-ranging support, inspiration, and patience during the lengthy development of this book, I would like to extend my deepest gratitude to Shannon Harvey, Prem Krishnamurthy, Rob Giampietro, Marina Kitchen, Kim Sutherland, Chris Wu, Aileen Kwun, Raquel Pinto, Scott Langer, Anna Mikkola, Kevin Wade Shaw, Meredith TenHoor, Christian Schwartz, Kevin Lippert, Jennifer Thompson, Sara Bader, Laurie Manfra, Deb Wood, Giovanna Borasi, Dan Wood, Irv Michaels, Margaret Michaels, Rachel Michaels, Andy Beach, Michael Worthington, and the Graham Foundation for Advanced Studies in the Fine Arts.

Published by:
Princeton Architectural Press
37 East Seventh Street
New York, New York 10003

For a free catalog of
books, call 1.800.722.6657.
Visit our website
at www.papress.com.

Special thanks to: Bree Anne
Apperley, Nicola Bednarek Brower,
Janet Behning, Fannie Bushin,
Megan Carey, Carina Cha,
Russell Fernandez, Jan Haux,
Linda Lee, Gina Morrow, John Myers,
Katharine Myers, Margaret Rogalski,
Dan Simon, Andrew Stepanian,
Jennifer Thompson, Paul Wagner,
Joseph Weston, and Deb Wood
of Princeton Architectural Press
—Kevin C. Lippert, publisher

INVENTORY BOOKS
Editor and designer:
Adam Michaels, Project Projects

PAP editor:
Sara Bader

This book has been generously
supported by the Graham Foundation
for Advanced Studies in the Fine Arts.

Library of Congress
Cataloging-in-Publication Data

Schnapp, Jeffrey T. (Jeffrey
Thompson), 1954–
The electric information age book :
McLuhan/Agel/Fiore and the
experimental paperback / Jeffrey
T. Schnapp, Adam Michaels.—1st ed.
     p. cm.—(Inventory books)
   ISBN 978-1-61689-034-6
   (alk. paper)
1. Book design—History—20th century.
2. Book design—Case studies.
3. Graphic design (Typography)—
History—20th century.
4. Paperbacks—Publishing—
History—20th century.
5. McLuhan, Marshall, 1911–1980.
6. Agel, Jerome. 7. Fiore, Quentin.
I. Michaels, Adam, 1978–
II. Title. III. Title: McLuhan/Agel/Fiore
and the experimental paperback.
   Z246.S267 2011
   686—dc23

                           2011020151K